MAKE YOUR OWN SCRATCH GAMES!

MAKE YOUR OWN SCRATCH GAMES!

ANNA ANTHROPY

no starch press

San Francisco

Printed in USA

First printing

23 22 21 20 19   1 2 3 4 5 6 7 8 9

ISBN-10: 1-59327-936-1
ISBN-13: 978-1-59327-936-3

Publisher: William Pollock
Production Editor: Laurel Chun
Cover Illustration: Josh Ellingson
Illustrator: Garry Booth
Developmental Editor: Annie Choi
Technical Reviewer: Kyle Reimergartin
Copyeditor: Anne Marie Walker
Compositor: Happenstance Type-O-Rama
Proofreader: Emelie Burnette

For information on distribution, translations, or bulk sales, please contact No Starch Press, Inc. directly:
No Starch Press, Inc.
245 8th Street, San Francisco, CA 94103
phone: 1.415.863.9900; info@nostarch.com
www.nostarch.com

Library of Congress Cataloging-in-Publication Data

Names: Anthropy, Anna, author.
Title: Make your own Scratch games! / Anna Anthropy.
Description: First edition. | San Francisco : No Starch Press, Inc., [2019].
Identifiers: LCCN 2019001474 (print) | LCCN 2019003410 (ebook) | ISBN
   9781593279370 (epub) | ISBN 159327937X (epub) | ISBN 9781593279363 (print)
   | ISBN 1593279361 (print)
Subjects: LCSH: Computer games--Programming--Juvenile literature. | Computer
   games--Design--Juvenile literature. | Scratch (Computer program
   language)--Juvenile literature.
Classification: LCC QA76.76.C672 (ebook) | LCC QA76.76.C672 A5845 2019
   (print) | DDC 794.8/1525--dc23
LC record available at https://lccn.loc.gov/2019001474

For the new generation, and
for the generation who grew up
without having the tools:
Here they are.

About the Author

ANNA ANTHROPY is a game designer, author, and educator. She lives in Chicago with her little black cat, Encyclopedia Frown, where she teaches game design as DePaul University's Game Designer in Residence.

About the Technical Reviewer

KYLE REIMERGARTIN is a parent and a second-grade teacher. He makes computer games, pies, zines, and tapes. Some of his favorite subjects to incorporate into his games include skin, places, rituals, doors, germs, teeth, and cats. He is the creator of *Fjords*, and he's currently developing a game called *Banana Chalice*, which will be finished in fifteen years.

Brief Contents

Contents in Detail

5 Creating Sound Effects 125

Acknowledgments

Thanks to Hax for making these books happen and to Caitlin for all she had to put up with. And to my perfect nebling Camilla Grace, for giving me a material reason to want these books in the world.

Everyone Makes Games

Video games can be playful, weird, exciting, curious, magi-
cal, and even downright scary. We enjoy playing games
because they act like windows into other worlds, worlds that
move and change as we play with them, worlds whose rules
are different than our own. (Sometimes these rules seem to
make more sense than our world's.) Games can be places we
visit for a short time or places we get lost in for long stretches
at a time. Through games, we can try on other personas and
explore different perspectives.

Whatever games might mean for you, you should know that you can make your own games. And it's a lot easier than you might think! The *Make Your Own Video Games* series shows you how to make fun, interactive games *from scratch* using a few tools.

What You'll Need

To create the games in this series, you'll need the following:

- Access to a computer
- An internet connection

That's it! In this book, we'll work with Scratch, a tool that makes it easy to draw characters that interact by snapping together simple code blocks to build fun, weird games.

Before you learn how to download Scratch and begin making your own games, let's first explore some history behind the games you enjoy today.

A Brief History of Games

Games have been around *forever*, or at least since the start of civilization. In fact, our oldest ancestors made their own games out of sheep's bones (the very first dice!). They used seeds and some holes in the dirt to make the game we now call *Mancala*. *Tic-Tac-Toe* was first played over 3,000 years ago in Egypt!

Games existed long before other activities, such as writing, painting, and 3D movies. It seems like people were born to *play*. Whenever a group of people agree to play by a certain set of rules, a new game is born. As these games pass on to new players, the new group puts its unique spin on it. For example, a *Tag* player might wonder, *Wouldn't Tag be more exciting if you could rescue people who've been tagged?* And just like that, a new rule is born: games grow and change over time like weird plants.

Games that are designed by a group of people instead of just one person are called *folk games*. No one person invented *Tag*. More likely,

Tag had a million different authors who each added their own little touches. This is why so many different versions of *Tag*, such as *Flashlight Tag*, *Freeze Tag*, and *Kick the Can*, exist today. All it took was someone to come up with another, more fun way to play the game, and the rest was history.

The mobile games on your phones are *designer games*, which were made by a single person or a team of people. They aren't folk games, but they're still the result of people playing games and trying to come up with different ways to improve a game or create new games using their imagination.

While playing a game, have you ever thought, *This game would be so much cooler if it just had this?* If so, congratulations! You are a game designer.

Who Makes Video Games?

In the 1960s, computers were the size of an *entire room*: these huge computers were called *mainframes*. Because computers were so expensive and complicated, only a few people could use them to make video games.

One of the oldest video games, *Spacewar*, was written by punching holes into paper cards and then putting the cards into a computer. After writing out the code on paper, you then had to figure out which holes to punch on a card so the computer could read and understand the cards. If any of the holes were wrong, you had to start over and repunch all the cards!

As you can imagine, computers were very tricky to use back then. They were also so big and expensive that only schools could afford them. In fact, most of the video games made in the 1960s and 1970s were designed by students at universities, such as the Massachusetts Institute of Technology (MIT).

But these students were not being taught game design in school. They were being taught serious computer programming. However, in between classes, they snuck away to the computer labs and figured out how to make video games because they thought games were cool. They disguised their games as Serious Computer Programs because the administrators would delete any programs that looked like games, calling them a waste of space.

Today, we remember some of those early games but not many of the Serious Computer Programs. Keep that idea in mind if someone complains about how much time you spend making games. People might forget the serious stuff, but they'll usually play a game for a very long time.

Computers have changed a lot since the 1960s. Now, you carry a computer in your pocket—your smartphone—which can do so much more than a huge mainframe computer ever could and is much faster. These pocket-size computers are also less expensive and easier to use.

You'll learn how easy it is to make your own video games using free, simple tools like Scratch, which hundreds of people have used.

These are people of different colors and genders, young and old. People who are sick and people who are well, those who have gone to college and those who haven't. People who like cats, people who like dogs, and those who like both. All kinds of people. So the answer to the question *Who makes videogames?* is *everyone*!

Why Make a Video Game?

People create video games for many different reasons. For example, maybe you've tried drawing comics, and it was fun. Maybe you've tried writing stories, and that was fun, too. Perhaps you enjoy arts and crafts as well as making music. Odds are, if you're creative, you'll also enjoy making games.

Another reason to create games is that you really like them and want to learn how they work. Making your own games is the best way to understand how game designers make decisions when they create your favorite games.

If you don't like games very much, that's okay, too! Perhaps you can make a new type of game no one has ever seen before—a game that is totally different from the currently available games. Gamers need to be challenged a little.

If you *already know* you want to be a game developer, you could try to make games that kids will love to play for generations, which will inspire *them* to make games.

For me, making games is exciting and new, even after all the time I've spent on them. Whenever I think I'm done, a new idea pops into my head. I can't stop thinking about it until it's out of my head And the only way to get the idea out is to make it a reality. When I create a new game, it feels like I'm creating something I can share with the world. It feels awesome!

There are a million and a half different reasons to make a game, and they're all great reasons as long as they excite you.

What Should My Game Be About?

Games can be about *anything*. Really, it's true. They can be about big things, small things, important things, silly things, people and places, your mom or dad, your brother or sister, or your cat or dog.

They can be about things that happened to you or things you *wish* had happened to you. You could make a game about your weird dreams, about a funny story you heard, or about robots taking over the Earth. Or perhaps your game can be about the network of secret tunnels leading from your basement to the center of the Earth (you know about those, right?) and the monsters that live in them. And the picnics they have down there.

You could just try re-creating games that you already play and like. Make your *own* game about the dude in the funny overalls with the mustache (Mario). For example, what would Mario do on his day off? Would he go on a picnic? Do you think he has a cat?

Although there are already games about almost everything, there is *always* room for more ideas. Don't let anyone tell you otherwise!

About Scratch

Scratch is a creative tool that was developed with kids in mind, but anyone can make games with it. It's easy to put together a simple game or animated story in Scratch. You can even draw your own characters and art directly into your project!

How Much Does Scratch Cost?

Scratch is free! Making your game, publishing your game, and putting it on the internet where other people can play it doesn't cost a thing. (Of course, someone in your home needs to pay for internet access, or you can try using a computer at your school or library.)

Do I Need to Know How to Program?

No, you don't need to know how to program! Scratch uses a system of simple building blocks similar to LEGO blocks that snap together to tell your game characters what to do. Because the blocks snap together only in certain ways, it's easy to tell where the blocks are supposed to go. Coding can be scary because sometimes your program might not work, and you'll have no idea why. But Scratch's snap-together system eliminates 90 percent of those situations.

What If I Already Love Programming?

If programming is your jam, you can really take off and run with Scratch. Although Scratch's snap-together blocks are simple and easy to use, they use the same ideas as any other programming language. Whether you know how to use branching, variables, loops, and so on or need to learn, Scratch is a great introduction to all of these concepts!

Alternative Tools

If you don't like Scratch, check out the two other books in this series: *Make Your Own Twine Games!* and *Make Your Own PuzzleScript Games!* Twine is ideal for telling stories with words, and PuzzleScript is best for making little puzzle-based games. But you should try to learn Scratch, too! The more tools you know how to work with, the more versatile you'll be as a creator. The best artists can pick up and use any tool to craft something that matches their vision.

1

Leaf Me Alone!: Scratch Basics

Scratch is neat tool for making animations, games, and movies. In this book, we'll focus on making games, so our projects will be playful and interactive. Scratch is mostly self-contained: for example, if you need a character for your game, you can draw it directly in Scratch or upload an image you already have. You can also choose one of the built-in Scratch characters.

We'll use Scratch's simple, block-based programming language to code the interactive parts of our game. Scratch uses a system of blocks that represent different functions. They snap together like puzzle pieces into complete lines of code.

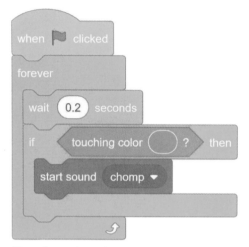

How Scratch code blocks fit together

These stacks of code blocks tell the objects in your games what to do. As you'll see shortly, using code blocks in Scratch is very easy.

Getting Started with Scratch

To begin, you need to sign up for your own Scratch account. It's free, and after you've registered, you can start saving and sharing your games. In your web browser, open the official Scratch website at *https://scratch.mit.edu/*.

On the Scratch website, click **Join Scratch** in the upper right. When asked, add your email address and some information about yourself. Then you'll get an email asking you to confirm your email address. Check your inbox and click the link in the email. Bam! You should now have your own Scratch account.

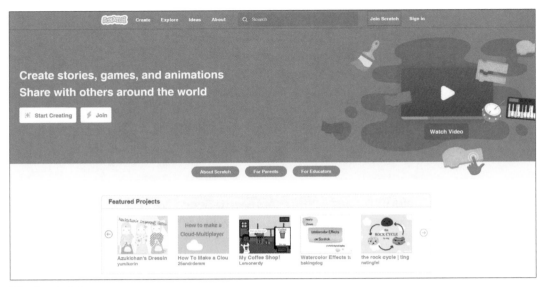

The Scratch home page

Click the **Create** button at the top of the Scratch home page if you're not already in Scratch's editor. You'll see a blank white box with a smiling orange cat, as shown in the following figure. This box is the game window, which is the only part of the editor your players will see. The cat is your first sprite. Let's talk about what a sprite is and what you can do with it.

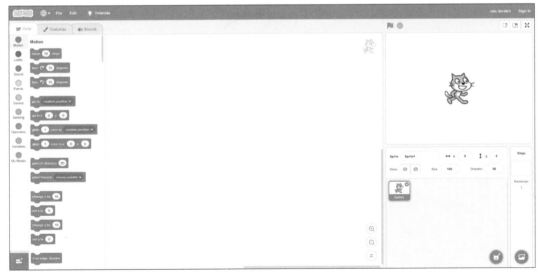

Opening the Scratch editor

That orange cat is Scratchy, Scratch's mascot. With every new Scratch project, Scratchy is automatically included in a noble effort to encourage more people to make games about cats.

Does Scratchy love lasagna? Does Scratchy hate Mondays? No one knows. But we *do* know that Scratchy is a *sprite*, which is any object in a Scratch game that can do something, like change its appearance or play music. Each sprite can have scripts, costumes, and sounds attached to it. A *script* is a group of coding blocks that fit together, telling the sprite what to do. A *costume* is a snapshot or a frame of a sprite that you can use to create animation. For example, the pose Scratchy is in right now is one of two default costumes that come with Scratchy. Click the **Costumes** tab on the top left (between Code and Sounds) to see the Scratchy sprite's costumes.

Scratchy comes with two costumes

When you flip between the two costumes by clicking one and then the other like a flip book, Scratchy should look they're walking. We'll use costumes to animate our sprites or change their appearance.

Sprites can also have sound effects that they can play. For example, Scratchy comes with a meow sound. Click the **Play** button in the Sounds tab to hear it.

Leaf Me Alone (While I Eat This Leaf)

We'll create a simple game in Scratch called *Leaf Me Alone (While I Eat This Leaf)*. It's about a hungry little bug who wants to eat a leaf and wants to do so in solitude. You can first play it at *https://scratch.mit.edu /projects/117199134/*, and then we'll create it.

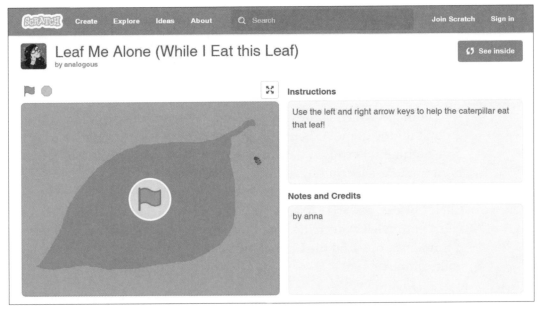

Exploring the Leaf Me Alone *game*

Click the green flag to start the game. The little bug starts moving forward automatically! Press the left or right arrows to make the bug change direction. As the bug eats the leaf, it leaves a trail of munches behind. This hungry little bug never stops munching. When you want to stop the game, click the red stop sign in the upper-right corner. If you click the green flag again, the game will start over.

It seems pretty simple, right? Now, let's make this game from *scratch*!

Creating Your Own Sprites

You'll need to draw your *own* sprites for the *Leaf Me Alone* game. One of Scratch's cool features is that you can use the mouse to draw characters for your game. Then you can give them instructions to make them do different things. It's okay if they turn out messy or imperfect. Don't worry!

Right-click Scratchy and click **Delete**. *Zoink!* Scratchy disappears. (You won't really hear a *zoink* sound. I made that part up.)

Next, look at the Sprites list below the game window.

Opening the Sprites list

The *Stage*, which is currently a plain white rectangle, is the background for the game. When you click it, it should be surrounded by a blue highlight. Because we deleted Scratchy, no sprites are in our Stage right now. Let's fix that by adding a new sprite!

Hover over the cat icon below the Stage to display four more buttons. Click **Choose a Sprite** to select a sprite from the Sprites Library. The Paint button lets you create your own sprite. The Surprise button selects a random sprite, and the Upload button lets you use an image from your computer.

Drawing Weird Bugs

Let's click the **Paintbrush** to draw a sprite for our game. Then click the **Costumes** tab. Now you're in the costume window where you can draw a costume for your new sprite.

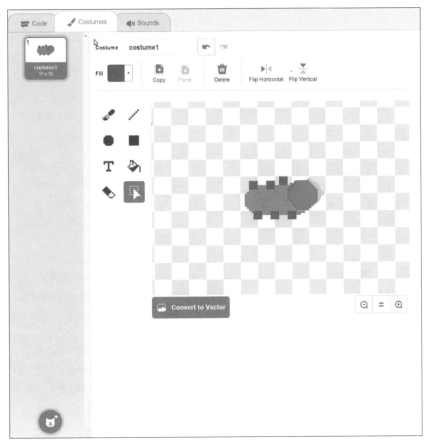

Drawing a new costume for your bug

On the left side of the drawing area is a menu of drawing tools. Make sure the paintbrush is selected. On the top of the drawing area is a color selector. To the right of the paintbrush icon is a number you can change to control the size of the paintbrush.

I drew a caterpillar, but you can draw any kind of bug you'd like. You should see a tiny plus sign (+) in the middle of the drawing area. That is the center point of the sprite: draw the bug's head there so its head is about the size of the plus sign (+).

That's a pretty small bug! To make drawing easier, use the magnifying glass buttons in the lower right to zoom in so you can see the bug better. The magnifying glass with the plus sign (+) zooms in, and the minus sign (–) zooms out. You can see what your sprite looks like at its normal size by looking over at the game window.

You can make your bug look however you want, but make sure it's facing toward the right. Scratch will automatically rotate your bug as it walks around the leaf, but sprites should always start by facing toward the right. So, if you want to give your bug a big weird butt, make sure its butt is pointing to the left side in the opposite direction of the head.

If you make a mistake while drawing your sprite, click the Undo button, which is the left arrow above your drawing. This button will undo the last change you made. If you decide you didn't want to undo the change, you can click the Redo button, which is the right arrow at the top of your drawing.

When you're happy with your bug, look at the Sprites list below the Stage again. Your bug should be there now, but it will be called empty. That's not the best name for a bug, but you can change it. Enter your new name into the Sprite field just below the stage. Change its name to something like weird bug or my perfect creation.

Drawing a Backdrop

The Stage is a lot like a sprite in that it also has its own scripts, costumes, and sounds. Costumes for the Stage are called *backdrops*. Any image you create for the Stage becomes the backdrop for the entire game window.

You can make multiple backdrops and switch between them at different moments in your game. For example, the first level of your game could take place in a forest, and the second level could take place underwater. For *Leaf Me Alone*, we need only one backdrop because there is only one level. Let's draw it now.

Click the **Stage** (the blank white rectangle) to the right of the Sprites list. The Stage should show the text 1 backdrop below it. Below that is a blue button with a stage icon that works just like the Choose a Sprite button. Hover over it to show four buttons that do the same things as the Sprite buttons but for backdrops.

Instead of making a new backdrop, we'll just paint over the empty white one we started with. If you're not in the drawing window, click the **Backdrops** tab. Let's draw the background for the game: a big juicy leaf for the bug to eat.

If you zoomed in to draw the bug, you might still be zoomed in. Click the button in between the two magnifying glasses (=) to go back to normal view. You should see the entire backdrop. If you can see sliders around the edges to scroll the view, it means you're still zoomed in.

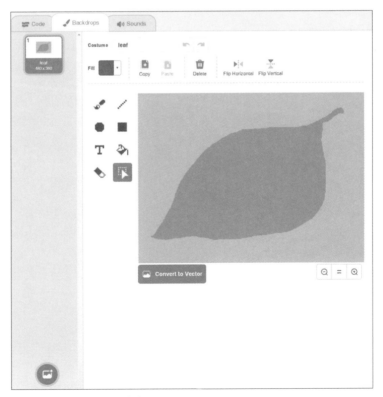

Drawing the leaf backdrop

We'll use two colors for this backdrop: one for the background and one for the leaf. (I used sky blue for the background and leaf green for the leaf.) Using just two colors here will be important when you write your program later, so make sure not to add more colors right now. You can also rename the background by clicking the text backdrop1 in the text field and entering a new name.

Now that we have our bug and our leaf, it's time to get our bug moving.

Using Event Blocks

Click your bug in the Sprites list, and then make sure you're in the Code tab. The empty area on the right is where we'll snap our code blocks together to write directions for our sprites. On the left are several categories that hold the different blocks that we can choose. Click a few of the categories to see which code blocks they contain.

For example, click **Events** to view the **Events** blocks, which let you sense events and trigger other code blocks:

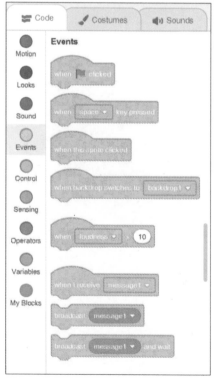

*Exploring the **Events** blocks*

Most categories are pretty self-explanatory. **Motion** blocks control movement. **Looks** blocks change the sprite's appearance. **Sound** blocks play sounds.

Every stack of programming blocks you'll write begins with an **Events** block. Click **Events** and you'll see that all the **Events** blocks have big round tops. Like a chef following directions to bake a cake, Scratch always reads directions from top to bottom. Keep in mind that an **Events** block *always* goes first; all other blocks can only attach underneath it.

Events blocks always go first (at the top).

Events answer the important question *When do I do this?* The **Events** block we want to use right now is when green flag clicked. Click and drag it into the area on the right.

Recall that you started the example game by clicking the green flag. The game had the when green flag clicked event, which tells the program to run the code blocks when the player clicks the green flag. Our game will start with this **Events** block too. Next, we'll write code that tells our bug to move.

Moving the Bug

Think of a bug crawling along a wall and the weird, winding path it takes. That kind of movement is very easy to replicate. The bug can keep moving forward until the player makes it turn to the left or right. To make our bug move, we'll use the blocks Scratch has for moving forward and turning. The player will have to do their best to guide the bug as it moves nonstop, making the game fun to play.

Let's start by making our bug move forward. The block that moves a sprite forward moves the sprite only one step forward. Because we don't want the bug to stop after just one step, we need to add a loop. A *loop* is a block that makes something happen more than once. To make our bug keep moving, we'll use a loop block to repeat a *move* instruction over and over for as long as the green flag is on.

Click the **Control** category to find all the blocks that handle *branching*, which is when you write different scripts that will run in certain situations. Think of branching code as branches growing off the main part of your code (the trunk). When different actions happen in your game, Scratch will make specific parts of the branch run. On their sides, branching blocks have empty slots in which to fit other blocks. For example, *looping* is a form of branching that can have different outcomes depending on the situation.

We want to use the simplest loop, which is a forever loop. Once a forever loop starts, it just keeps running over and over until the game is over. We use a forever loop because we want our bug to keep moving as long as the game is running. Click and drag a forever loop to attach it to the bottom of the when green flag clicked block. A shadow of the block should appear to show you can connect it.

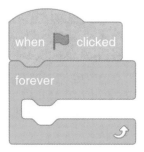

*Attaching a **forever** block*

You can put as many other code blocks inside a forever loop as you want. The loop runs the blocks inside it in order from top to bottom and then jumps back to the start of the loop to repeat them. The forever loop continues repeating the loop until you click the stop sign to end the game.

We'll add a move () steps block into the forever loop to move our bug forever. You can find this block in the **Motion** category. We'll also add a block that prevents the bug from moving off the Stage, because the player won't be able to see the bug and it might get lost. So, we'll add an if on edge, bounce block to the loop that makes the bug change directions when it hits the edge of the Stage.

Click **Motion**. Click and drag the move 10 steps and if on edge, bounce blocks into the forever loop.

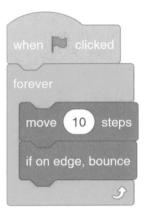

Creating a motion loop

The move 10 steps block makes a sprite take 10 steps in the direction it's currently facing. Double-click the number **10** to change the number of steps the bug will move. A lower number makes the bug move slower. I changed the number of steps to **5**.

Click the green flag to test your code. The bug should start moving to the right until it hits the edge of the Stage; then it will reverse direction and walk back to the left, then reverse toward the right again. And on and on.

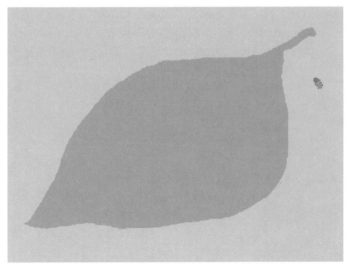

Testing your bug's movement

While your game is running, a glow should appear around the stack of code blocks you just made. The glow indicates that the bug is currently following the directions in that stack. For example, if you didn't have a forever loop, the glow would disappear after that stack of code was finished running. You can use this glow to keep track of which parts of your code Scratch is running at any given time and to help make sure all parts of your program work properly. The glow comes in handy when you try to debug your code later on!

Steering the Bug

Our bug can move only in a straight line, but we want the player to use the arrow keys to turn the bug left and right. First, we need to check whether the player is pressing a key that makes the bug turn. Second, when we know which key the player is pressing (left or right arrow), we need to make the bug turn in the correct direction.

We'll use branching again as well as an if () then block to check first whether the player is pressing a key; then (and only then) will we make our bug turn. Again, all the blocks related to branching are in the **Control** category.

Click and drag an **if () then** block and place it under the if on edge, bounce block inside the forever loop. We put the if () then block in our forever loop so the player can turn the bug as long as the game is still running.

Using an if () then block

The hexagonal hole in the middle of the if () then block holds **Sensing** blocks. **Sensing** blocks check whether a specific action has happened, such as whether two sprites are touching or whether a player is pressing a key. The **Sensing** blocks are pointy and hexagonal, just like the hole they fit into. Click and drag the **Sensing** block if key space pressed? and place it into the hole in the if () then block.

Because the space key isn't the key we want to check for, click the small black triangle next to it and choose **left arrow** from the drop-down menu. The block should now show if key left arrow pressed? then.

When the player presses the left arrow key, we want the bug to turn left! In the **Motion** category, find the turn left 15 degrees block. It should have a counterclockwise arrow on it. Drag that block over and snap it onto the bottom of the if key left arrow pressed? then block. The space between the two blocks should light up to show you where the connection will be. Finally, change **15** to **10** in the turn left 15 degrees block to make the left turns a little less sharp.

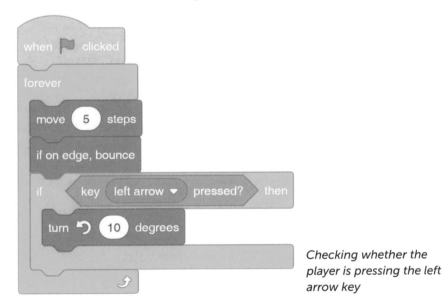

Checking whether the player is pressing the left arrow key

Run the game and see if you can make your bug turn in circles by holding down the left arrow key! Now let's make the bug turn right as well.

Right-click the if key left arrow pressed? then block and select **duplicate**. A copy of that block including the turn left 10 degrees block inside it should appear under your cursor. Place that copied if () then block below the preceding if () then block.

```
when ⚑ clicked

forever
  move 5 steps
  if on edge, bounce
  if  key left arrow ▼ pressed?  then
    turn ↺ 10 degrees

  if  key right arrow ▼ pressed?  then
    turn ↻ 10 degrees
```

Checking whether the player is pressing the right arrow key

Be sure to click the black arrow next to left arrow and change it to **right arrow**. Then remove the turn left 10 degrees block by clicking and dragging it back into the block list on the left side. Next, find the **Motion** block turn right 15 degrees (it has a clockwise arrow). Place this block inside the if key right arrow pressed? then block and change the number to **10** (otherwise, the bug will turn right at a different angle than it does when turning left).

Test your code again, and make sure pressing the left arrow key turns the bug left, pressing the right arrow key turns the bug right, and pressing neither makes the bug move straight.

If you hold down the right arrow key and the bug turns left, you forgot to replace the block inside the if key right arrow pressed? then branch! If the bug keeps turning, even when you're not holding down an arrow key, you put the turning block in the main forever loop instead of inside the if () then branch! Check your code blocks against the ones shown in the book to make sure all your blocks are in the correct places.

Chewing Holes in the Leaf Using Pen Blocks

Now our bug is moving all over the leaf, but it's not really wreaking a path of destruction yet. Let's make it chew its way through the leaf, leaving a trail of bite holes behind it!

To do this, we'll use the **Pen** blocks. Imagine a mass-produced room-cleaning robot with a marker taped to it that moves in a straight line across your kitchen floor, scaring your cat: the device would leave a line on the floor behind it, showing where it moved. (Don't try this at home!) Just like this cleaning robot, a sprite can use a pen to draw on the backdrop.

We'll draw the color of the sky onto the leaf, making it look like the bug has chewed holes through it. That's why it was important to make the background behind the leaf just one color!

To add the **Pen** blocks, click the blue button at the bottom-left corner of the screen. This should pull up a library of Extensions. Click the **Pen** extension to add it. We need to place all the **Pen** blocks *before* the forever loop, not inside it, because we want them to happen only once at the start of the game. Think of this part of the code as the setup area.

Add the set pen color to block. We'll set the pen color to the color of the sky by clicking the colored box in the set pen color to block, clicking the dropper at the bottom of the menu that pops up, and then clicking the backdrop of the Stage. Add the set pen size to block and change the size to **5** because that seems like a reasonable size for the bug's mouth. Then add the pen down block to start drawing, similar to lowering a pen to paper. (The pen up block stops drawing.)

Notice that there is a set pen size to as well as a change pen size by block. *Setting* makes the pen size a specific value, such as 1, 10, or 187. *Changing* adds a number to that pen size. If the pen size is 1 and you use a set pen size to 1 block, the pen size is still 1. If the pen size is 1 and you use a change pen size by 1 block, the pen size is 2 because you've added 1 to 1. Don't get them mixed up!

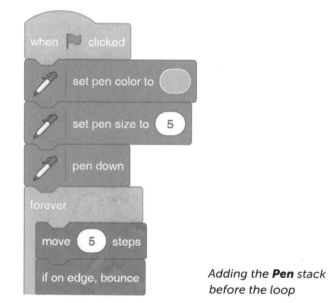

*Adding the **Pen** stack before the loop*

After you have all your **Pen** blocks in place, click the green flag. The bug should now leave a trail through the leaf as it chews. Using the arrow keys, try making the bug chew big, curving lines.

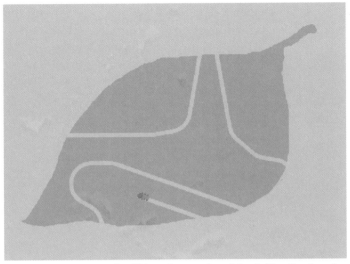

The bug leaves a trail of blue that makes it look like the bug is chewing through the leaf!

Our bug is making lines through the leaf now, but the lines look a bit too neat and smooth to be holes left behind by a hungry bug. Let's make the line a little *chompier* by changing the line as it's drawn.

Click another set pen size to block (*set* not *change*) and drag it into the forever loop, as shown here.

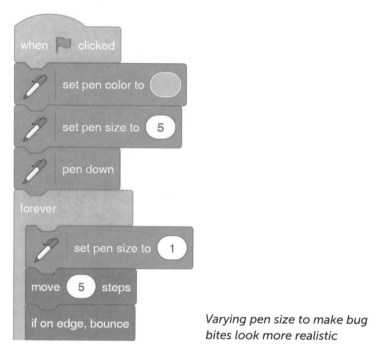

Varying pen size to make bug
bites look more realistic

We want the set pen size to block inside the forever loop so we can change the size again and again, every time the bug moves. We'll change it at random.

You already know that you can change a number that is in a hole in a block by entering another number. Well, some Scratch blocks can also calculate numbers using the numbers you fill in. Those blocks are in the **Operators** category, as shown here.

Operators blocks

Operators blocks perform mathematical operations. Any rounded block can fit into a round hole in any other block (including other rounded blocks!). The first four blocks perform simple mathematical functions: addition, subtraction, multiplication, and division. We'll use the fifth block: click pick random 1 to 10, and drop it directly over the number **1** on the set pen size to 1 block, as shown here. Any rounded block can fit into a round hole in any other block (including other rounded blocks!).

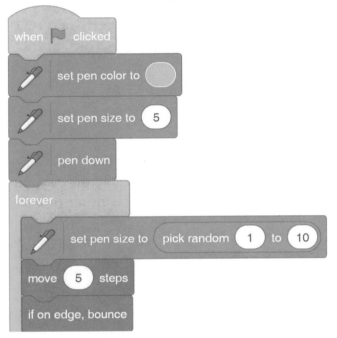

Randomizing pen size

The pick random operator picks a random number between the two numbers you specify. In our code, the number could be between 1 and 10 but could also include the numbers 1 and 10. With this block as part of our forever loop, every time the bug moves the pen size will change.

Now the trail that the bug leaves should look like it's made up of individual bite marks because each chomp will be a slightly different size. Click the flag and see what happens!

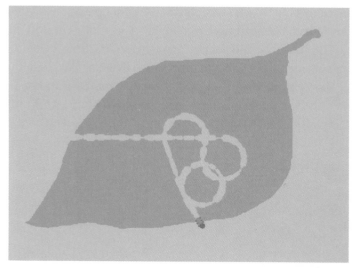

Using randomized pen lines to make bug bites look more realistic

The new lines look chompier—*nice*!

But notice that all the old chomp lines from the bug's previous meals still appear. They never go away! Let's add some instructions to make sure the game starts with a clean leaf every time we run it.

Starting Fresh Each Game

To refresh the game each time it starts, we'll add three blocks to the setup part of our code: the part before the forever loop starts. The setup code runs once when the game starts and never again until the game starts over.

The first two blocks we need to refresh our game are the **Motion** blocks go to x: y: and point in direction. The two blocks make sure the bug always starts in the same position. The third block we need is a **Pen** block called erase all, which we'll use to clear the trail the bug drew in the previous game.

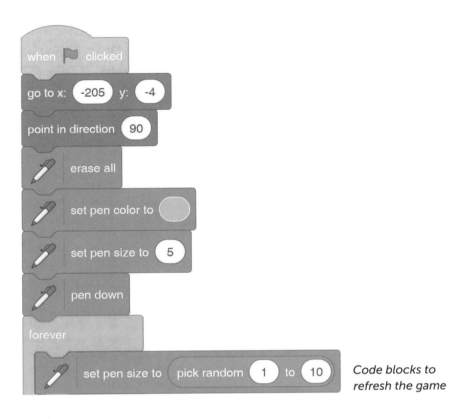

Code blocks to refresh the game

Using the Grid

The go to x: y: block moves a sprite to any position on the screen, which you define using two numbers *x* and *y*. In Scratch, we use numbers on a grid to locate the position of different objects. Imagine an invisible grid over the Stage. This grid is made up of two number lines that intersect at the center of the screen. The numbers on the horizontal line (*x*) increase to the right and decrease to the left. The numbers on the vertical line (*y*) increase up the line and decrease down the line. Any numbers to the left of the center point on the horizontal number line or below the center point on the vertical line are negative.

The value *x* is the sprite's place along the horizontal line, and *y* is its place on the vertical line. Every possible position on the screen has an *x*-coordinate and *y*-coordinate that indicates how far it is from the center of the screen. For example, in the bottom-right corner of the game screen, you'll see the x- and y-coordinates showing the current position of your mouse. Watch how these numbers change as you move your mouse around the screen.

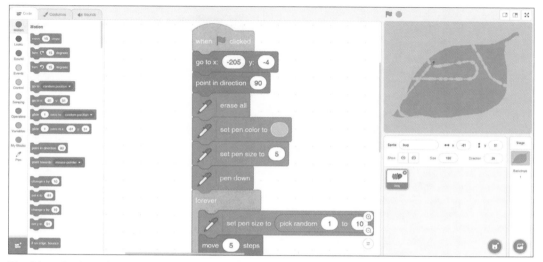

Tracking the location of your mouse with x- and y-coordinates

Setting Your Bug's Starting Position

The go to x: y: block always starts with the current position of the sprite. (Try dragging and dropping the bug in different places on the screen; the numbers in the go to x: y: block will change.)

An easy way to set the bug's starting position is to first drag the bug to wherever you want it to start at the beginning of the game. Then drag the go to x: y: block into your stack in the setup area. The coordinates of the bug's current position will be filled.

Setting Your Bug's Starting Direction

The go to x: y: block sets the bug's starting position but doesn't affect the bug's starting direction. To set the bug's starting direction, you need to use the point in direction block. Click the triangle on the point in direction block and, from the drop-down menu, choose **90**, the direction we want the bug to start in.

Every direction has a number associated with it. In Scratch, when the bug turns, its direction number changes. The direction number is the angle the sprite is facing. Imagine a circle that has a number line wrapped around its circumference with the sprite positioned in the middle of the circle. The sprite's direction at 0 means it's facing straight up (the very top of the circle). Each number is called a *degree*, and the angle of the circle can range from 0 to 360 degrees. As the degree number changes, the sprite changes the direction it's facing. For example, 90 degrees changes the sprite's starting direction to the right, which is the direction we want the sprite to face when the game starts.

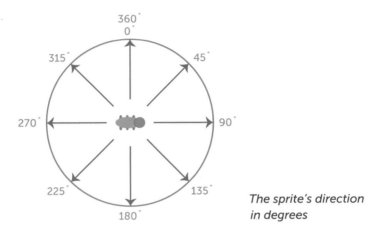

The sprite's direction in degrees

Resetting the Background

The erase all block clears all the pen marks that have been drawn so far, making our leaf pristine and new again. Place the erase all block directly below the go to x: y: block and point in direction block at the beginning of your stack so they run first when a player clicks the green flag.

Click the green flag to run the game and make sure all the blocks work. Click the flag a few more times to reset the game each time. Your game should start in the same condition every time.

Checking for Contact Between the Bug and the Leaf

To really sell the idea that the bug is tearing right through this leaf, let's play a munching sound effect whenever the bug is chewing on it. To do that, we first need to check whether the bug is touching the leaf. If we played the sound *all the time*, whether or not the bug was on the leaf, it wouldn't match what was happening onscreen. So we want to be sure to check for contact between the bug and the leaf.

To check for contact, we'll use one **Control** block and one **Sensing** block to branch our code when the bug is on the leaf, just like we checked for a left or right arrow keypress earlier. To keep our stack neat, we'll add a second when green flag clicked block instead of adding to the existing one. As a result, we'll have two identical stacks that begin with the when green flag clicked block.

Creating two stacks like this works well. In fact, you can have as many identical events as you want. When you click the green flag to start the game, *all* the when green flag clicked events will run at the same time. You'll find this technique useful when you want to run multiple loops with different timings or when you just want to organize the code, like we're doing now.

Start the new code stack by clicking and dragging a new when green flag clicked block from **Events.** Put it next to the other one, creating a new stack. Then give it its own forever block. We use the forever block because we want the bug to keep checking whether it's touching the leaf during the entire game. Inside the forever block, place an if () then block.

To check whether the bug is touching the leaf, add the if touching color ? then block inside the if () then block. When you click the colored box in the block, a menu pops down; click the dropper and then the leaf, and the color in the box should change to the color in the leaf.

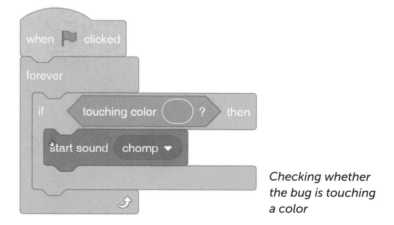

Checking whether the bug is touching a color

Because we drew the leaf using just one color, we only have to check that the bug is touching that color. Next, we'll add the sound we want to play inside the branch.

Playing Sounds

Click the **Sound** blocks category and drag the play sound pop until done block into the if touching color ? then branch. In Scratch, sprites come with the pop sound by default. You can click the Sounds tab to play the sound.

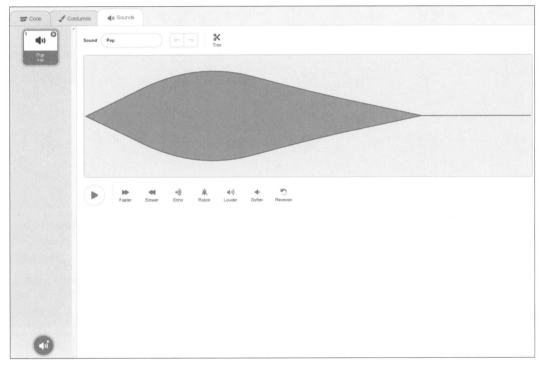

Playing the pop sound effect

A sprite can have multiple scripts and costumes attached to it, and it can have multiple sounds as well. Right now the only sound our bug has is pop, but that's not a sound a bug might make while eating a leaf. Let's find a better sound.

Scratch comes with a huge library of sound effects, such as beatboxing, animal sounds, and music. Click the **Choose a Sound** button to add a sound. Hover over it to display the other options. The Record button lets you record a sound, the Surprise button selects a random sound for you, and the Upload button lets you upload a sound from your computer.

← Back			Choose a Sound			

🔊	🔊	🔊	🔊	🔊	🔊	🔊
A Bass	A Elec Bass	A Elec Guitar	A Elec Piano	A Guitar	A Minor Uk...	A Piano
🔊	🔊	🔊	🔊	🔊	🔊	🔊
A Sax	A Trombone	A Trumpet	Afro String	Alert	Alien Creak1	Alien Creak2
🔊	🔊	🔊	🔊	🔊	🔊	🔊
B Bass	B Elec Bass	B Elec Guitar	B Elec Piano	B Guitar	B Piano	B Sax
🔊	🔊	🔊	🔊	🔊	🔊	🔊
B Trombone	B Trumpet	Baa	Bark	Basketball ...	Bass Beatbox	Beat Box1

Exploring the Sound Library

You'll find a ton of sounds in the Sound Library! Click the **Animals** category to narrow the list down. Listen to sounds by hovering over them. Try to find a bug munching sound. When you find a sound you like, double-click it to add it to your sprite's sounds. Try the chomp sound for this example.

Now that your bug has its new sound effect, return to the Code tab. Click the triangle on the play sound until done block to change the sound from pop to chomp. Your bug should now play the chomping sound effect while eating the leaf. Run the game to hear what it sounds like!

It sounds a little weird—definitely not the same as the preview! The game plays the entire sound effect only *after* the bug moves off the leaf. The reason is that the bug tries to play its sound whenever it's in contact with the leaf; however, the sound restarts *every moment* the bug is in contact with the leaf, down to a fraction of a second. So it sounds like a continuous drone instead of a series of distinct sounds. We need to use the **Control** category's wait block to make the bug wait just long enough for the entire sound effect to play before replaying the sound.

Drag the wait 1 seconds block into your stack, just above the if () then block. Place it *before* the branch, not inside it. Otherwise, it will check whether the bug is touching the leaf *and then* wait one second before playing the sound.

One second is a bit too long between chomps. Instead, let's try using **0.2** seconds, which is two-tenths of a second. One complete second is a surprisingly long amount of time in a game!

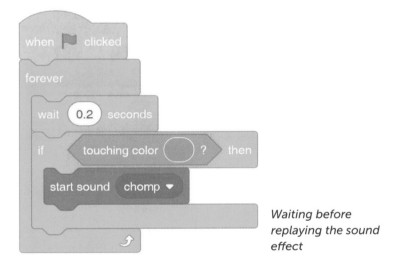

Waiting before replaying the sound effect

Run the game now. With a 0.2 second delay between chomps, the chomps should sound a whole lot better. *Chomp chomp chomp chomp chomp chomp chomp.*

Organizing Your Code

Our game is basically complete, but let's take a moment to think about how best to lay out the Code area visually. Where should you put the instructions for your sprite in the Code area? Blocks need to be connected in the right places or they won't work correctly.

Right now, I'm not talking about situations where there's an obvious right answer. I'm talking about the decisions that don't affect how your code runs, but *do* affect how it looks when someone is reading it. For example, when you use two different when green flag clicked stacks, where should you place them? Do you put one below the other? Or perhaps side by side?

This question is about form, not function. It's entirely a matter of personal preference. It doesn't matter to Scratch whether two stacks of code are above and below each other or side by side. They could be on top of each other in a messy heap, and as long as the code blocks are connected in the right ways, Scratch will still run them. So, does it matter where you place your stacks of code?

Well, yes, it does! Your Code area is like the inside of your head. The way you organize the Code area reflects your thought processes and how you think about your game. When the Code area is disorganized, your thoughts are jumbled and hard to follow. If one of your players clicks the **See inside** button to look at how you did something in your game, how you arranged your scripts will make a big difference in whether or not it makes sense to them.

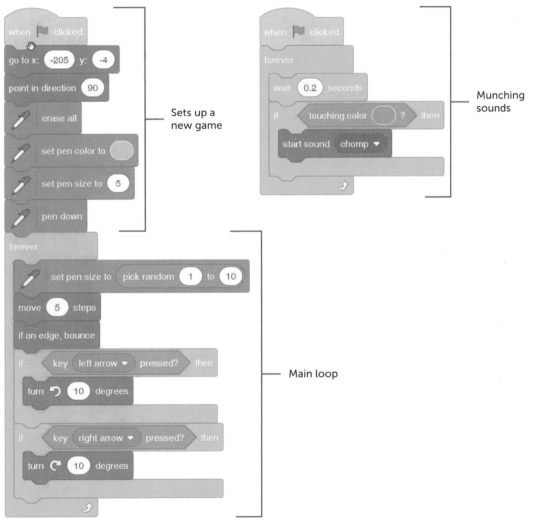

Organizing the Leaf Me Alone *code stacks*

A thoughtful layout can help you keep your thoughts in order, help you remember what all your script parts do, and help make your script clearer to others who look at your work.

Placing related stacks next to each makes the most sense to me. For example, putting the when green flag clicked events next to each other is logical because they start at the same time and run simultaneously.

Scratch offers a couple of helpful functions for organizing your code. When you right-click the coding area, you can click **Clean up Blocks** to arrange all your stacks neatly, or you can click **Add Comment** to attach a note to your code. You can even attach a note to a specific block by right-clicking on the block and choosing **Add Comment**. Comments help explain the block's purpose in the game to others (and help you remember what the block does). Comments don't change how the code runs—they just make it a lot easier for humans to understand!

The layout of your game doesn't have to match my layout exactly. But the layouts you use should make sense to you. Think of rearranging the stacks in your Code tab as a way of organizing your thoughts.

Challenge Level

With the Scratch knowledge you have now, try this optional task: make your bug burp after it has eaten some leaf. To make this work, you'll probably want to use the following:

- A forever loop to make sure the burp is not a one time effect
- A **Sensing** block to check whether the bug is on the leaf
- A wait block to make sure the burp doesn't happen too often
- A little randomness to keep the game interesting
- A burping sound (Try recording your own burp sound using the microphone on your computer. Do your best pretend burp!)

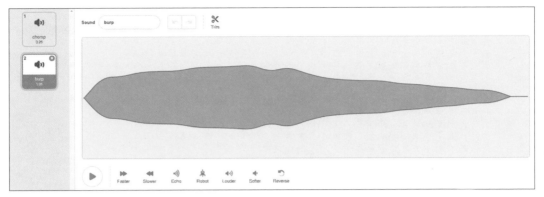

Recording your own burping sound

If you need help completing this task, click the **See inside** button on *Leaf Me Alone* to see how I did it! (Not the burping sound, just the code.)

Sharing Your Game

All you need to do now is share your game with the world! Right now, no one can see your game except you. You can tinker with it as much as you want—no one's looking! After you've shared your game, other people can find it and play it, so make sure you've made all the changes and final touches you want before sharing it. But don't worry; you can keep changing it after you share it or just temporarily unshare it again to make changes.

There are two buttons at the top of the Scratch editor: Share and See Project Page. Don't click Share just yet. You still need to do a few more tweaks before you make your game public.

Click **See Project Page** to go to the page your players will see when they look at your game.

Leaf Me Alone (While I Eat this Leaf)

See inside

Instructions

Use the left and right arrow keys to help the caterpillar eat that leaf!

#Games #Animations

Notes and Credits

by Anna Anthropy

♥ 0   ★ 0   ◎ 0   ◉ 1   Mar 14, 2019   + Add to Studio   Copy Link

✎ Pen

Comments   Commenting on ⬤

The See Project Page

At the top of this page is a handy reminder that you've not yet shared the game. You should fill out the Instructions to tell players how to play the game (for example, "Use the left and right arrow keys to help the caterpillar eat that leaf!"), and add the Notes and Credits (for example, your name or "my finest creation!").

Use a hashtag (#) to create a link to the search results for that word. For example, try adding your username, the title of your game, or words like *games* and *animations* as keywords to help others find your game.

When the game is complete, click **Share**. Now people on the Scratch site can find your game, or you can share it with a friend by giving them the link. You've finished your first game!

One last detail: click your username in the top right, and then click **My Stuff** in the drop-down menu to go to your personal My Stuff page. The My Stuff page keeps track of all your projects, finished and unfinished, shared and unshared. You can also see how many people have looked at your game, sort through all your projects, and even unshare a game you've shared by clicking the Unshare link.

+ New Project   + New Studio

Sort by ▾

All Projects (1)

Shared Projects (1)

Unshared Projects (0)

My Studios (0)

Trash

Leaf Me Alone (While I Eat this Leaf)
Last modified: less than a minute ago

Add to ▾

See inside

👁 1   ⊘ 0
💗 0   ★ 0
💬 0   🗂 0
Unshare

Load More

Viewing all your projects on the My Stuff page

Think of the My Stuff page as your personal, secret headquarters. From here, you can unleash all your diabolical Scratch plans on the unsuspecting masses! Or, you can just keep track of every project you're working on.

What You Learned

You learned a bunch of good stuff in this chapter! You used Scratch's block-based programming to create backdrops and sprites for a game. You also learned how to use loops, how to take input from a player, and how to use conditionals and branching. In Scratch, you can use x-coordinates and y-coordinates to keep track of where your sprites are onscreen. You know how to share your game when you finish it and how to use the My Stuff page to keep track of all your cool projects.

In Chapter 2, we'll make a game that becomes more challenging as the player improves. We'll also talk about more advanced programming ideas, like coding sprites to clone themselves. See you there!

Weird Bug Chowdown: Collecting Items and Avoiding Obstacles

Let's take the little leaf game we've made and turn it into *Weird Bug Chowdown*, which has more of a story arc. Instead of making a game about a bug just munching a leaf forever, this game will start easy, get harder, and eventually reach an ending. We'll talk about some of the most common elements in video games—collecting and avoiding things! We'll also explore time pressure, one of the most fundamental features of real-time games.

You'll also learn a few more Scratch features, such as the following:

- Using clones to create more sprites
- Creating and keeping track of your own variables
- Creating your own events and using them to send messages between different sprites
- Using a little bit of animation

You can play *Weird Bug Chowdown* at *https://scratch.mit.edu/projects /117389078/*.

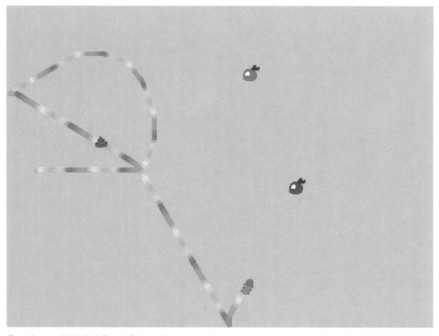

Preview of Weird Bug Chowdown

This weird bug wants to get as big as possible by eating all the berries! But berries go bad if the bug doesn't eat them fast enough. Also, every time the bug eats a berry, it leaves something stinky behind that you probably want to avoid. Can you reach the end of the game? (It's kind of hard, so if you can't get to the end, try making your version easier.)

When you've played enough, let's dive in and start making the game!

Copying a Project and Changing It

This time, let's not start from . . . scratch (you know what I mean). Instead, let's build on our previous project by copying it to a new project. Open *Leaf Me Alone* by clicking **See inside** either on the My Stuff page or on the game's Project Page.

If you haven't created your own version of *Leaf Me Alone* yet, find the game at *https://scratch.mit.edu/projects/117199134/*, and then click the **Remix** button in the upper right to get your own copy to work with.

Creating a copy of Leaf Me Alone

Once you have a version of *Leaf Me Alone* saved as a remix, click **File ▸ Save as a copy** to create a copy of the game to work on. Its new name should look something like "Leaf Me Alone copy." Click the name to change it to **Weird Bug Chowdown** (or an even better name).

Saving a copy of Leaf Me Alone

Because we're starting with an existing project, we already have a loop that moves our bug forward and events that let the player turn left and right. We'll tweak these for the new game we'll make.

Weird Bug Chowdown requires some bug maneuvering skills where the player chases tiny berries while avoiding hazards at the same time. To make the bug a little easier to maneuver initially, let's change its move speed to 3. Now it should move 3 steps during its loop instead of 5.

Tidying Up Your Code

Because we don't need the leaf-crunch noises, we'll remove that whole stack from the Scripts area. Click the **when green flag clicked** block at the very top to select all the other blocks in that stack, and then drag it out of the Scripts area. (Make sure you get rid of the shorter stack that makes chomping noises, not the one that moves the bug!)

We'll also take the left and right turning branches out and make them their own when green flag clicked stack, as shown on the next page.

Making two stacks of code is an optional step to prevent the stack with our main loop from getting so long that it won't fit on the screen. Don't forget to give the new stack its own forever loop, too. Sometimes, this kind of tidying up can help you keep track of your code. Now you'll know whether each stack of code is for the setup and main game loop or for pressing buttons and turning.

```
when [flag] clicked
go to x: -205 y: -4
point in direction 90
[pen] erase all
[pen] set pen color to ( )
[pen] set pen size to 5
[pen] pen down
forever
    [pen] set pen size to (pick random 1 to 10)
    move 3 steps
    if on edge, bounce
```

```
when [flag] clicked
forever
    if < key left arrow pressed? > then
        turn ↺ 10 degrees
    if < key right arrow pressed? > then
        turn ↻ 10 degrees
```

Reorganizing our existing stack

Before we start working on our new game, let's make one more small change to the code that we have.

Leaving a Rainbow Trail

For this game, let's use the pen for a neat rainbow effect instead of leaf eating. Then our bug will leave a rainbow trail behind it wherever it goes. Because this game is all about wiggly bug movement, it would be cool to see exactly where your bug has been while playing it.

Let's modify the main loop so the bug draws a little differently.

First, we delete the set pen color to block. Because we'll cycle through all of the colors of the rainbow, it doesn't matter what color we start with.

Then we add a set pen saturation to 50 block to make the colors more saturated because we want the rainbow super light and pastel. If you set the saturation to 100 instead, you would get a super dark rainbow. Setting it to 0 makes it all white.

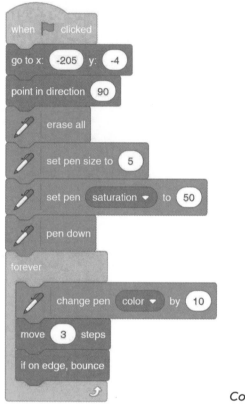

Code to leave a rainbow trail

The final and most important change is getting rid of the set pen size block inside the loop (the one that creates the random hole bite effect) and replacing it with a change pen color by 10 block. This block produces the rainbow effect.

In Scratch, the pen color, like the x- or y-coordinates, is just a number. By adding to or subtracting from this number, we can change the color the bug is drawing with. By using a bigger or smaller number, we can change how quickly the rainbow cycles through the colors. We use 10 here, but experiment to find the one you like best.

We also got rid of the leaf in the background by creating a new backdrop image and deleting the old one. (You can do this from the Backdrops tab after clicking on the Stage.) Use a solid background color for the rainbow to show up against. If you're feeling ambitious, you could draw a whole new background. But the rainbow effect will make the background interesting to look at on its own so it doesn't really need anything extra. Everyone loves rainbows! What could be better?

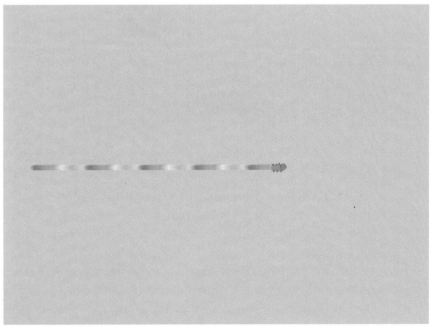

Testing the rainbow trail

Making Bug Food

Now let's make some berries for our bug to eat. Click the **Paint** button that looks like a paintbrush on the sprite menu.

Draw a berry and make it a little red circle right on top of the + that's not much bigger than the bug. You can add a little leaf on top and a little white spot to show where the light is shining on it.

When you're done, click the **Sprite** box in the bottom-right corner (it'll be called Empty) and change its value to **Berry**. Change the value of the costume name (in the upper-left corner, by the undo buttons) to **costume1**. Now what do we want our berry to do?

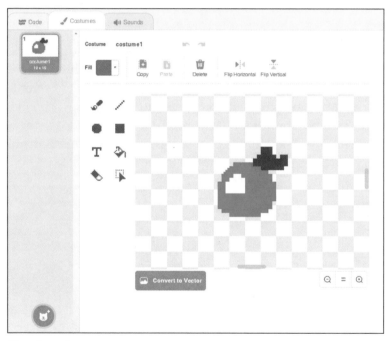

Drawing a berry

Let's think for a moment about the role of objects like this in games. Many games have coins, rings, gems, or other things the player is supposed to collect in tricky-to-reach places. But what do they actually *do* in those games?

In *Weird Bug Chowdown*, the berries give the player something to *do* with the ability to control the bug's movement. Objects like berries can motivate players to understand how the bug moves and challenge them to get better at controlling it.

We'll have the berries pop up at random places on the screen so the player can try to move the bug to them. How do we make multiple berries? The most obvious way is to make multiple berry sprites. But even if we made, say, five of them, and they were all identical, we'd still only have five of them. Plus, if we ever wanted to change the code in one of them, we'd have to change it *in all five of them*. That's way too much work. Instead, we'll make just *one* berry sprite that can *clone* itself.

Making a Sprite Clone Itself

A clone is just a copy of a sprite that the sprite produces while the game is running. Any sprite can make a clone of itself at any time if it's programmed to do so. Clones are not individual objects with their own code. We code them by coding the original sprite, and then telling it what to do when it's cloned using a few special blocks made just for clones. Note that clones disappear when the game is over.

First, we'll program the berry sprite to teleport to a random position on the screen and then clone itself. The cloned berry will sit and wait for the player to try to eat it. Then the original berry will wait a few seconds, teleport again, and make *another* clone, and so on. The original berry will just teleport around and produce clones, and the clones will be the berries the player eats. Let's see what this looks like in code.

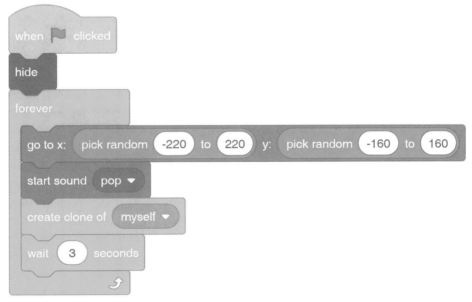

Code for making self-cloning berries

First, the berry *hides* because this original berry is only here to make clones. The player should only be able to see the clone berries. (The hide block is under **Looks**.) When it becomes invisible, it starts its loop. It moves to a random position on the screen, plays *pop* (the sound effect every sprite starts with), and clones itself. It pauses three seconds between each cloning and then starts the loop again, producing a new clone at a random position. (All of the clone-related blocks are under **Control**.)

Using Negative Numbers

The go to x: y: block sets x to a random number between –220 and 220 and y to a random number between –160 and 160. These numbers come from the coordinate system talked about in Chapter 1.

When you move your mouse around the game area and watch the x- and y-coordinates in the corner, the numbers get smaller toward the middle. The center point of the screen is point 0, 0. If you move to the right, the x number gets bigger up to 240. If you move to the left, the numbers get lower. Numbers less than 0 are *negative numbers*.

Negative numbers are like a mirror image of the regular numbers, so if you subtract 1 from 0, you get –1, and if you subtract 100 from 0, you get –100. Like normal numbers, the further they get from 0, the bigger the number gets. The furthest left x position is at –240, which is the mirror of 240 on the right. The y position goes from 180 at the top of the screen to –180 at the bottom.

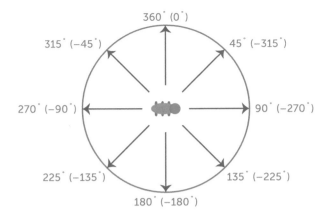

360° (0°)

315° (−45°)   45° (−315°)

270° (−90°)   90° (−270°)

225° (−135°)   135° (−225°)

180° (−180°)

Creating a Berry-Free Zone

If we set x to pick random -240 to 240 and y to pick random -180 to 180, we'd cover every possible position on the screen. So why use −220 to 220 and −160 to 160 instead? Because the bug bounces off the edges of the screen, we don't want the berries to appear too close to an edge, making them unfairly difficult to collect. To avoid that, we create a comfy buffer of 20 berry-free coordinates around the edge of the screen by subtracting 20 from 240 and 180 to get 220 and 160.

Try running the game now. You probably won't see anything, but you should hear a popping sound every three seconds. This is because the clones are all invisible right now. Because the original berry *hides* before it clones itself, the clones also start as invisible berries!

Because the berry's clones are created *after* you click the green flag to start the game, they don't have the when green flag clicked event. That's a good thing because otherwise they would be teleporting around and cloning themselves like the original berry, and soon the screen would be covered with berries. When you're working with clones, it's best to use the when green flag clicked event for only stuff you want the *original* sprite (not the clones) to do. We'll use a special event to write code for things we want *only clones* to do.

> **NOTE:** Remember that clones disappear when the game stops running, so don't worry about invisible berries clogging your game.

It's time to give those clones something to do. They can begin by making themselves visible again.

Telling a Cloned Berry What to Do

We'll use the when I start as a clone event to tell the clones what to do. Even though it's an event, you'll find it under **Control** with all the other clone-related blocks. The event when I start as a clone lets you write code exclusively for clones. The original sprite will never see this event. Whatever comes first inside the when I start as a clone block will be the first action the clone takes after it's created.

The first thing our berry clone does should be to make itself visible with the show block, which is in the **Looks** category.

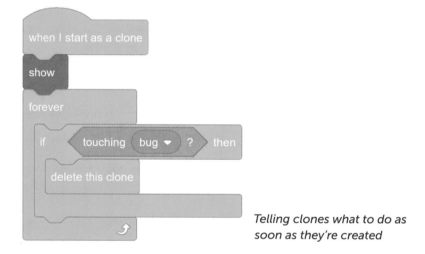

Telling clones what to do as soon as they're created

Because we can create as many clones as we want, we can also get rid of them. This ability is useful; otherwise, clones could get out of hand! To get rid of clone berries after a bug has eaten them, we use a conditional to first check whether the berry is touching the bug. If it's touching the bug, we delete it to show that the bug has eaten the berry. Make sure this check happens inside a forever loop so the berry can keep checking for the condition.

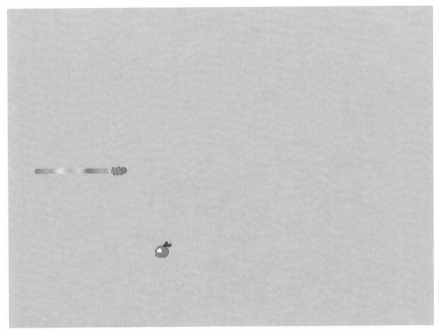

Testing whether berries pop up

Try running the program! Every three seconds, a new berry should appear on the screen and disappear when the bug touches it. How quickly can you eat the berries?

Broadcasting Messages

Having the berries just disappear when the bug eats them is a little anti-climactic. Instead, let's make the bug grow a little bigger every time it eats one. To do that, we'll need a way for the berry to send a message to the bug, telling it that the bug has eaten the berry. When the bug gets the message, it'll run a special event that tells it to grow bigger.

In Scratch, this is called broadcasting and receiving messages. When a sprite *broadcasts* a message, that message is sent to every other sprite in the game simultaneously. Any sprite with a when I receive event for that message will run whatever code is attached to that event after receiving the message. Sprites without an event for that message will ignore it. It's like when you post a picture on Instagram. You're sending it out to the entire world, but only the people who are following you on Instagram will see it.

You can find all the blocks related to broadcasting and receiving messages under **Events**, as shown here.

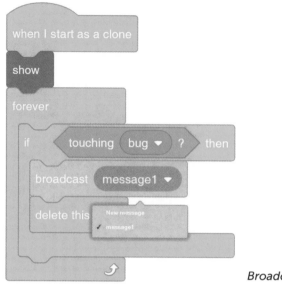

Broadcast drop-down menu

Drag the broadcast message1 block into your if touching bug branch, right above delete this clone. We want the berry to check whether it's touching the bug, send the bug a message, and then disappear. The default message is message1, but you can change which message the berry sends by clicking the triangle on the broadcast block. Click **New message** to create a new message called yum.

Now click the bug and give it a new stack that starts with the when I receive yum event. You might have to click the triangle on the when I receive yum block and change the message to yum.

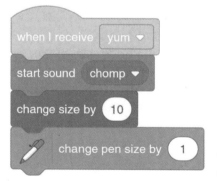

Creating the when I receive yum block

Now when the bug gets the yum message, it can play its chomp sound effect and grow a little bigger. Let's also make the pen size bigger, so the bug's rainbow trail gets larger as the bug gets larger.

Make sure you also add a set size to 100% block to the bug's setup code (in the when green flag clicked stack) so it resets its size when you restart the game! Otherwise, the bug will keep getting bigger and bigger forever (100% is a sprite's original size).

Now try eating some berries and watch your bug and its rainbow trail grow! *Nom nom nom.*

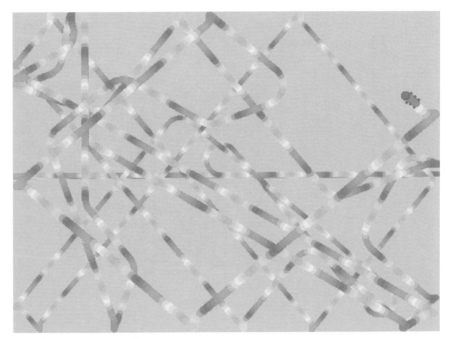

Watch your bug grow!

Adding Time Pressure

From the moment the player clicks the green flag, time is ticking in our game. As game designers, we should think about how we make use of time. For example, we can decide how much time the player should spend in a level, how much time should pass before the monster starts chasing the player, or how much time the player has to grab a winged ball before it flutters out of reach. Time is an amazing tool when we use it deliberately.

When the timing is too slow, players could get bored because they don't feel much urgency. When the game moves too fast, players feel like they can't possibly keep up. In either case, they disengage because nothing they do feels like it has consequence.

But if we use time thoughtfully, we can keep the energy of the game moving by keeping up the momentum. For example, in *Weird Bug Chowdown*, berries appear every three seconds. Players need to use the right *timing* to turn the bug at just the right moment to gobble up a berry. But they have as much time as they want to collect a berry, and the berries stick around forever.

Right now, players have all the time in the world to collect berries, so there's not much forward momentum in this game. But what if we added *time pressure* by making berries turn bad if the bug didn't get them in time, like a fruit going bad after being left on the counter for a week? Then the player would have a reason to try to grab them as soon as they appear.

We could also make the bad berries reverse the player's progress, turning the bad berries into obstacles the bug would have to avoid. This would create pressure to eat the berries quickly and consequences when the player isn't able to do so.

Let's talk about how to make a good berry go bad.

Using Animation to Make Bad Berries

To make the player understand the berries are going bad, we need a way to show it to them. We also need to show how close a berry is to going bad to give players time to react. Visuals are a great way to communicate information about the state of the game.

We'll make different costumes for the berry so the player can watch it change color as it gets closer to becoming a bad berry. Then we'll flip through the different stages of berry ripeness, creating a little animation.

Drawing Costumes

Open the berry's **Costumes** tab. Right now, the berry has a single costume (give it the name costume1 by typing the name into the box next to the undo arrows). Right-click that costume and choose **duplicate** to make a copy of that costume called costume2. Don't change costume1. We'll draw some big purple spots on costume2, making it look like it's halfway through the process of turning from red to rotten purple.

Right-click **costume2** to make another duplicate, which is costume3. Use the paint bucket tool to add more purple spots in the remaining red on costume3. Now the berry is completely purple.

Duplicate costume3 to make costume4, and draw some blue spots on it for a blueish purple berry. Then make costume5 completely blue to make a berry that is going bad.

Drawing costumes for your berry

We want a visible transition from color to color as the berry grows closer and closer to its final, rotten form. Here, we drew seven costumes, starting at solid red before turning purple, then blue, and eventually blue with big gross green splotches in costume7, which shows the kind of berry you wouldn't want to eat.

By looking at the color of the berry's costume at each stage, the player should know how close the berry is to being inedible. Red is perfect, purple is halfway to going bad, and blue is getting nasty. Green and splotchy is rotten.

Coding the Animation

Let's look at how we tell the berry clones to cycle through all the costumes.

We need two separate events using when I start as a clone for each. One checks for contact with the bug. The other event handles all the visuals, like making the berry visible, resetting its appearance to costume1, and then animating it.

Because these stacks involve different timing (one uses a forever loop, and the other uses wait and repeat), they can't be in the same stack. Whenever two pieces of code have different timing like this, we must put them in separate events, even when both events start at the same time. Then they won't get in each other's way.

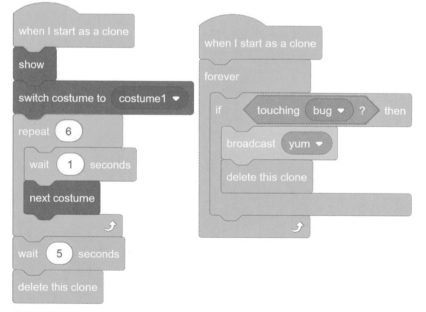

Animating how your berry goes bad

In the visual stack, we use a repeat 6 loop to advance through the costumes with one second between each costume change. The repeat block is like the forever block, except instead of repeating the branch inside it forever, it just repeats it the number of times you specify. We use repeat 6 here because there are only six frames until the final frame that shows the gross splotchy berry (costume7).

After the repeat block runs the specified number of times, Scratch exits the branch and moves on to whatever code is below it. In this case, that code waits another five seconds and then deletes the clone. That way, rotted berries stick around long enough to be an obstacle, but don't hang around forever. Otherwise, the game would get too hard.

Run the game and watch your berries go bad.

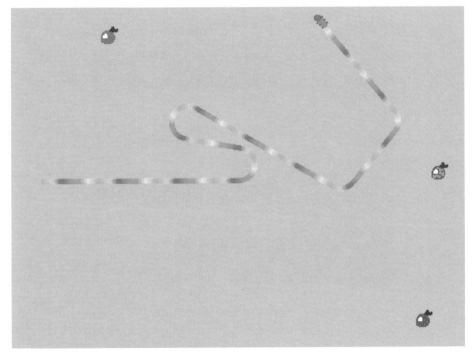

Testing to see how the berries go bad

When a berry pops up, the player has six seconds to eat it before it goes bad. That's just enough time to reach a berry from anywhere on the screen. Then it stays bad for another five seconds until it finally vanishes. But right now, you can still eat berries after they go bad with no consequences. We haven't made them do anything different when they go bad. Let's do that next.

Branching with if and else

We used if () then blocks to check whether the bug was touching the leaf or a berry. Now we'll use if / else blocks to decide whether the berry is good or bad when the bug touches it. The if / else block (under **Control**) has two branches: one for the if and one for the else. If the condition is true, the code in the first branch runs, and if it's not true, the code in the second (else) branch runs.

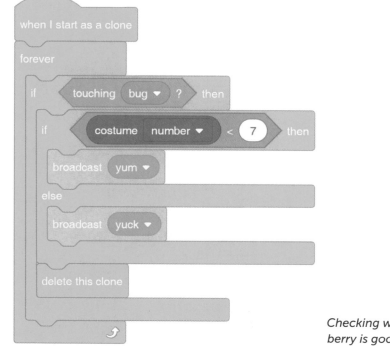

Checking whether a berry is good for eating

Let's unpack this stack to understand it. The first outermost block is a forever loop, because we want this berry to continually check whether the bug is touching the berry. Nestled inside the forever loop is the if touching bug block that performs the check. First, we check that the bug is actually touching the berry, and only *then* check what kind of berry it is.

The next level down is the if / else block: if costume number < 7 then broadcast yum, else broadcast yuck. The costume number (under **Looks**) just shows the costume number the sprite currently appears as. The < symbol means "is less than," which checks whether the costume number is less than 7. You can find the < block under **Operators**.

The bad berry costume is costume7. We want the bug to take one action if the berry's costume number is 7 and another action if it's less than 7.

If the costume number is between 1 and 6, the berry is still good to eat, and we broadcast the yum message. Or *else* if the costume number is 7 and the berry is bad, we transmit the yuck message by clicking the triangle and then **New message**.

Regardless of whether the berry is good or bad, we need to *delete this clone*. Removing the berry is not part of the if / else block and happens after that block is evaluated. We want the berry to disappear whether it's healthy or not.

That's it for the berry.

Recording the yuck Message

To make the bug receive the yuck message and react accordingly, we'll record a new sound by saying "eww" into the microphone. When the bug receives the yuck message, the game plays that sound and then the bug gets smaller.

When the bug eats a good berry, it gets bigger by 10, so we'll shrink the bug by 10 as well. We can shrink the bug by telling it to get bigger by –10, which is the same as saying it gets smaller by 10. We also make the pen smaller, to match the bug's new size.

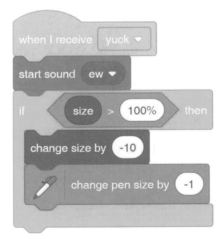

Making the bug say "eww" when it receives the yuck message

We add the conditional if size > 100% before the size change to make sure the bug can't get any smaller than its starting size. (Keep in mind that 100% is a sprite's starting size.) If we don't set this conditional, the bug could shrink out of existence just by eating too many bad berries!

Let's test our game. Try to make the bug get bigger, and then shrink it back to its original size. Check that the bug can't get any smaller than its starting size.

Poop Obstacles

Now our game has obstacles for our bug to avoid. More importantly, the bug knows what to do when it collides with an obstacle. When it receives the yuck message, it follows the code in its yuck stack. We can use the yuck stack to add other obstacles, too. All we have to do is make new obstacle objects broadcast yuck messages when the bug touches them.

I have the perfect object in mind for a new obstacle: poop! Hear me out: bugs poop when they eat, right? My professional background is not in insect digestive systems, but bugs most likely poop sometimes. Using poop would be a fun way to tie all of the existing game elements together: the bug, the berries, and the consumption of said berries.

When the bug eats a berry, it'll digest the snack for a second, and then a little poop will appear behind it. This poop works just like a bad berry does. If the bug touches its poop, it broadcasts a yuck message and the bug gets smaller. Avoid the poops!

Why Poop Obstacles Work

The poop obstacle will never appear *in front of* the bug. The berries pop up at random positions and sometimes appear right in front of the bug where the player can't possibly avoid them. But the player *wants* to collect berries, so that's like a free bonus. If poop obstacles appear in front of the bug, that would be unfair.

Because the bug's poop always appears behind the bug, it helps the game's forward momentum. The bug is continuously moving forward, so the poops give the player a reason to avoid retracing their path, pushing them to always explore other parts of the screen.

Another selling point for creating poop as an obstacle is that everyone playing your game already understands how it works. Everybody poops and instinctively knows to avoid it.

Making Poop by Having Sprites Clone Other Sprites

To create our poop obstacle, hover over the **Choose a Sprite** menu, click the **Paint** button, draw something gross, and rename the sprite poop. If poop grosses you out, you can make your bug lay weird bug eggs instead or leave chewed-up little berries behind it, like tiny apple cores. No one wants to touch those!

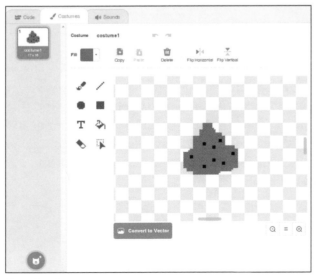

Drawing bug poop

Here are some tips for drawing good poop: click the little rainbow-looking box next to the palette below the drawing zone to get more colors to choose from. The slider to the right of this new rainbow palette lets you make colors brighter or darker. If you darken the palette a little, you should be able to pick a nice poopy brown. To make it look even grosser, set your drawing size to very small and draw some tiny black specks on the poop. There. Magnificent!

Coding the Poop Obstacles

Unlike with the berry, we won't have the poop clone itself. Poops don't appear on their own; they appear from the bug after it eats a berry. So we'll tell the bug to make the poop clones using the create clone of myself block. Click the triangle next to myself and change it to poop.

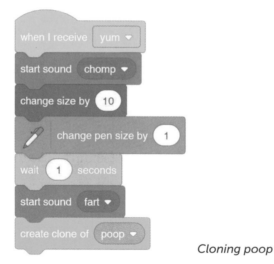

Cloning poop

The bug makes a clone of the poop as part of the when I receive yum event. Add a wait 1 secs block and a play sound block and then set the sound to fart. Now, when the bug eats a berry, it'll change its size as instructed, digest for one second, play a farting sound, and produce a poop clone. (You can record the farting sound by blowing a raspberry into the microphone.)

Now let's use when I start as a clone events to tell the poop clones what to do after they appear.

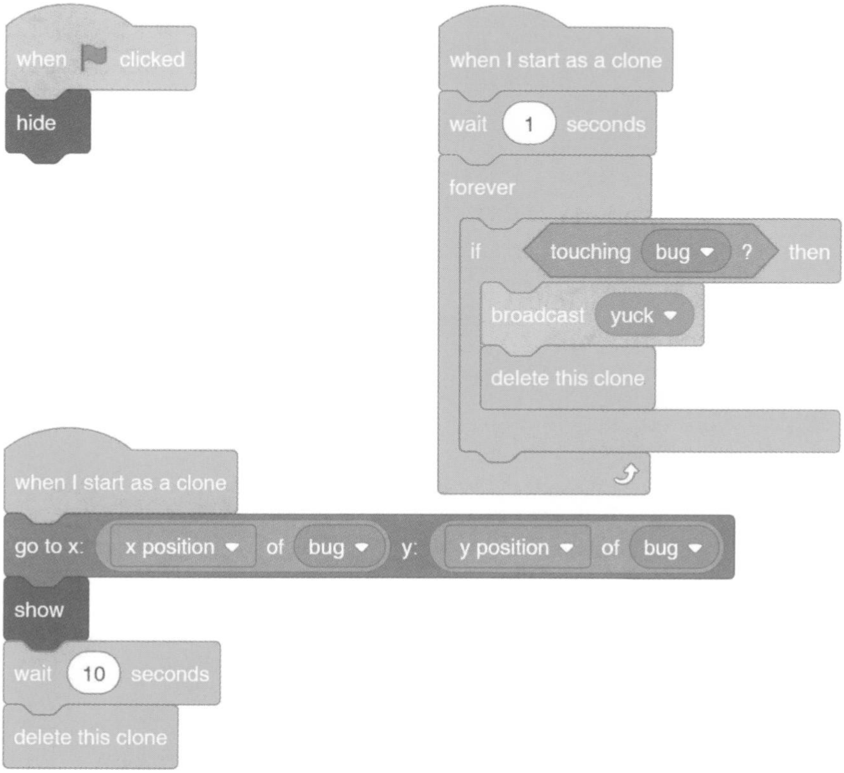

```
when [flag] clicked
hide
```

```
when I start as a clone
wait 1 seconds
forever
  if < touching bug ? > then
    broadcast yuck
    delete this clone
```

```
when I start as a clone
go to x: (x position of bug) y: (y position of bug)
show
wait 10 seconds
delete this clone
```

Code that tells poop clones what to do

The poop code is split into three stacks. The reason is that the timing of the forever loop and the wait 10 seconds block need to run in their own stacks. Also, the when green flag clicked, hide stack should only run when a new game is started. Here is what each stack does:

Hides original poop   The first stack makes the original poop sprite disappear, because we only want poop to show up in clone form.

Makes poop appear behind the bug The when I start as a clone stack in the lower left makes the poop start at the same x and y position, just like the bug. (You can find the x position block under **Sensing**.) Without this teleportation block, the new poop would appear wherever the original poop sprite was hidden instead of appearing in the bug's trail. Then we tell the poop clone to *show* itself, wait 10 seconds, and then delete itself. Poop, like all things in life, is temporary. If it wasn't, the game would get way too hard.

Checks for poop contact The when I start as a clone stack on the right checks for a poop clone's contact with the bug. When the bug touches the poop, the poop broadcasts yuck and deletes itself. This is pretty much the same as with a bad berry. But notice that it waits one second before it starts checking for contact with the bug. That's because each poop starts at the same position as the bug. If it didn't wait a second before checking, the bug would smash into it as soon as it appears. *Gross.*

Run your game. Check that the poops appear, that they go away, *and* that they work as obstacles when the bug bumps into them. Poops galore.

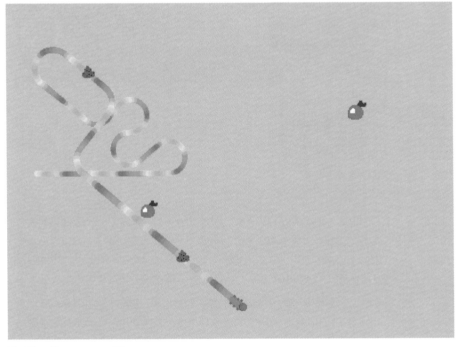

Testing the game with poop

Raising the Stakes

Now our game is full of exciting objects. The bug has items to collect and obstacles to avoid, like bad berries and poop. But maybe our game would seem more complete if it had more of a story and if there was escalating tension as it went on? For example, what if the better the player did, the harder the game became? Right now, the bug gets bigger as it eats, which makes it a little bit harder to avoid obstacles as the game progresses. But it doesn't make the game that much different to play. What if the bigger the bug was, *the faster it moved*?

That way, the better the player is doing, the trickier the game gets. If it gets too hard and the bug hits some obstacles, it'll shrink and the game will get slower and easier again. Adding this game play allows the game to meet the player's skill level.

Creating Our Own Variables

To keep track of the bug's speed while it's moving, we'll need to use a variable. We've already used variables: when we tell a sprite to go to x 100, we're changing its x variable. When we change the color of a sprite's pen, we're changing a color variable. We can also create our own variables and use them to keep track of whatever we want, like the bug's speed.

Click the **Variables** category in the Code tab, and then click **Make a Variable**.

Creating a new variable for speed

Name your variable **speed** and set it to **For this sprite only**. That just makes it easier to keep track of, because only the bug needs to know what speed it's going.

After you name and create your variable, Scratch generates some new blocks to help you work with it.

The first new block is a round value block, which you can put into any slot in a block that wants a value. In this case, we'll use the bug's current speed as the value. There are blocks to set a variable to a specific number or change it by adding a number as you would for any other sprite property, like direction or costume number. Then there are blocks that show and hide the variable. What do those do exactly?

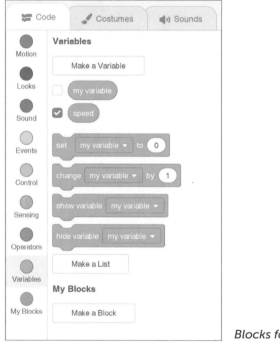

Blocks for your new variable

You should see a check mark box next to the speed value block. If that's checked, you should see a little display in the corner of your game that shows the value of the speed variable while you play.

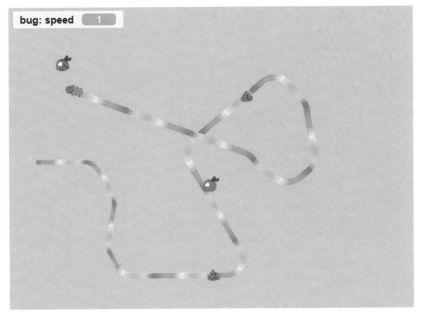

Showing a speed display

This display can be useful while testing your game. You can see your variable's value at any given time, so you can make sure it's working as expected. When you uncheck the box, this display goes away. You'll probably want to uncheck the variable before sharing the game. But sometimes you might want to leave a variable visible in a finished game. For example, if the display shows information you want the player to know, like their current score or the number of cupcakes they've collected, you'll keep it visible.

Let's use the speed variable blocks to change the bug's speed as the game goes on.

Changing Speed

Using the speed variable is pretty simple. First, make sure the bug's speed is set to 0 in its setup phase, before the main loop starts.

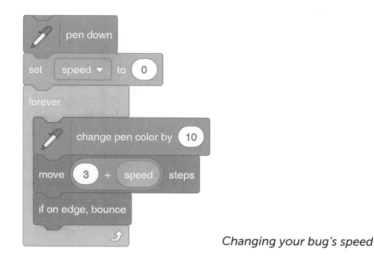

Changing your bug's speed

Then let's change how far the bug moves after every run through the loop. To move our bug by 3 + speed steps, you'll need to grab the addition block, + , from **Operators** and drag the speed value block into the second slot of the + block. The minimum speed will be 3, which is the bug's current speed. The speed variable, which starts at 0, keeps track of how much speed the bug gains on top of its starting speed.

Now we have a starting point from which to increase the bug's speed every time it eats a berry and decrease when it hits an obstacle. We'll do that using the change speed by block.

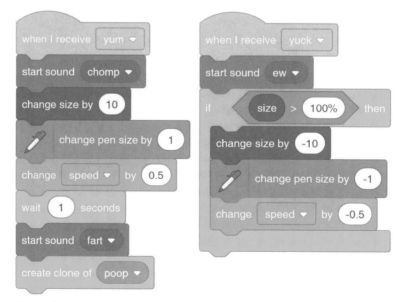

*Using the **change speed by** block*

A good increment is 0.5 seconds, which is half of 1, or five-tenths of a second. If the increment was 1, the bug would speed up too quickly. Try different numbers. Check the speed display in the corner to make sure that eating berries makes the bug faster and hitting obstacles slows it back down again.

Ending the Game

The bug in *Weird Bug Chowdown* gets bigger and faster the more berries it eats. But right now, there's no real limit to how big it can grow or how fast it can go. The bug would just keep growing and growing. We can pick a point in the bug's growth and say, that's enough! We can make something happen when the bug gets to a certain size or is moving at a certain speed. For example, when the bug is really huge, instead of getting any bigger, it could turn into a butterfly.

How do you decide what the endpoint is? How fast is too fast? Turn on the speed display and play the game for a bit. Try to find the point where it's fast, difficult, and intense, but not *too* fast, difficult, and intense. Find the point *right before* the game would get too hard, and remember the speed variable number. For me, 7.5 feels like a good top speed.

We want the game ending to be big and splashy. When the player reaches the game's end, they should know it and feel rewarded. But before we code it, let's pick a new costume to represent the bug's evolved form and add a little music to play during its transformation.

Choosing the Butterfly Costume

Go to the bug's **Costumes** tab. You can draw your own new costume for the bug if you want, such as a multicolored butterfly that is way bigger than the original bug (but still facing to the right!). For this example, I'll pick a butterfly costume from Scratch's built-in library.

Hover over the costume menu and click the **Choose a Costume** button to bring up a menu of pictures. This should look similar to the Sound Library we picked the chomp effect from. Again, you can click the **Animals** category to make it easier to find the butterflies. I like Butterfly2-b because it's the most colorful yet still weird looking. A weird bug would grow up into a weird butterfly, wouldn't it?

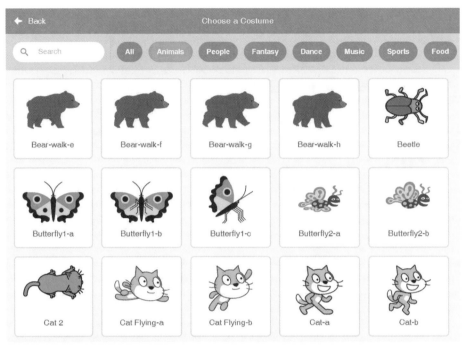

Choosing a butterfly costume

Let's pick some music to accompany the transformation. Again, we'll dig up something from the Sound Library. Check out the **Loops** category to find a bunch of short music pieces. We'll use the one called dance magic. It sounds like music you might hear while transforming into a butterfly.

Coding the Metamorphosis

Using simple branching, we'll code the transformation. When the bug eats a berry, we use a conditional to check whether the bug is fast and big enough to transform. If the bug hasn't reached its size and speed limit yet, the game continues and the bug just gets bigger and faster. (We'll use speed 7.5 to check whether it's moving at that speed.) If it's fast enough, we'll broadcast the new message evolve.

```
when I receive  yum ▼

start sound  chomp ▼

if       speed  =  7.5       then

    broadcast  evolve ▼

else

    change size by  10

        ✎    change pen size by  1

    change  speed ▼  by  0.5

    wait  1  seconds

    start sound  fart ▼

    create clone of  poop ▼
```

```
when I receive  evolve ▼

switch costume to  butterfly3 ▼

set size to  100  %

go to  front ▼  layer

set  speed ▼  to  0

set  evolved ▼  to  1

start sound  dance magic ▼
```

Turning your bug into a butterfly

As you can see, we made a when I receive evolve event to handle the actual transformation. Yes, this means that sprites can receive messages that they can also broadcast! We can use a broadcast to make a sprite run an event in the middle of another event. This evolve event changes the bug to the butterfly costume and sets its size back to 100%. Otherwise, it would be super huge, because the bug is over double its starting size at this point!

Then the event sends the butterfly to the front. "Sending it to the front" means bringing it closer to the screen than the other objects. Think of a pile of photos sitting on your kitchen table. We want the butterfly to be in front of all the other sprites so it can soar over them on its majestic wings. If we don't send it to the front, the clone berries and poops would look like they were in front of the butterfly, which would be odd.

Then the event changes the bug's speed back to 0 (so it drifts gracefully instead of zooming superfast), sets a new variable called evolved to 1, and plays the dance magic tune.

The variable evolved keeps track of whether the game has been won. When you create the evolved variable, be sure it's a For all sprites variable. We want every sprite in the game to be able to tell whether the game is over.

New Variable   ✖

New variable name:

evolved

● For all sprites   ○ For this sprite only

Cancel   OK

Creating the evolved variable

We can also use the evolved variable to give the butterfly a cool color-changing effect. Under **Looks**, the change color effect by block changes how the sprite looks. You can set this block to do a bunch of different effects, like whirl, pixelate, and ghost, which makes a sprite see-through.

To create a colorful butterfly, we'll use the color option. This option changes all the colors of the sprite to other colors, similar to how we created the rainbow effect by cycling through the pen's color.

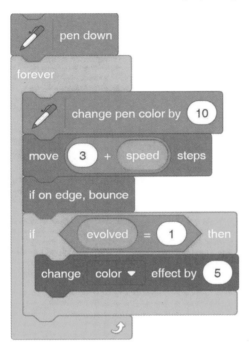

Changing the butterfly's color

In the bug's main loop, use a conditional to check whether the evolved variable is equal to 1. If it is, run the color effect. Normal movement, drawing, and bouncing off the edge of the screen should still happen, so we don't want to change that.

It's important to make sure your bug changes its costume back to its original, weird bug form during its setup phase. Add the switch costume to costume1 block and the set evolved to 0 block to the when flag clicked event. Both blocks will reset the variables that are changed in the butter-fly ending. Otherwise, you could start the game as a butterfly when you restart the game!

All right, try your game to see if it works. Can you get to your game's ending and turn the bug into a butterfly?

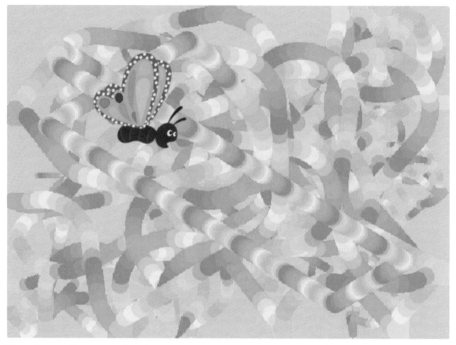

Transformation complete!

Changing the Butterfly's Behavior

If you're able to turn your bug into a butterfly, you'll notice that the butterfly can still eat berries, poop, and get bigger or smaller. The butterfly is supposed to be the bug's final form that transcends a bug's mortal limitations. It's also supposed to be flying in the air where it should no longer have to worry about poop or bad berries.

Because we made evolve a *universal variable*, which is a variable that all objects can see, we can just add conditionals to berries and poop to prevent them from checking for collision with the bug after it has evolved. Here's what the conditional looks like for the poop sprite.

We check whether the evolved variable is equal to 0, which means that the bug has not yet evolved into a butterfly. Only *then* do we check for contact with the bug.

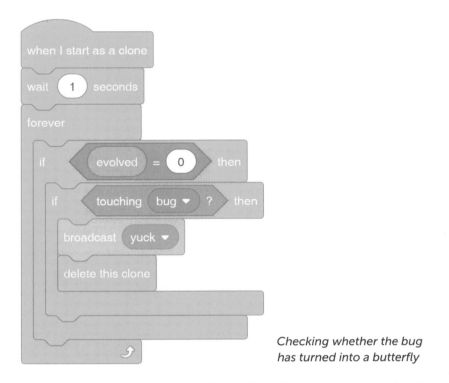

*Checking whether the bug
has turned into a butterfly*

You can use the same conditional on the berry: use one conditional to keep the original berry from making clones after the player has won. Use another conditional to keep clones from checking for contact with the bug after it has turned into a butterfly. Just make sure your blocks are nested correctly.

Most importantly, be sure that everything that should only happen before the bug has evolved is *inside* the branch instead of outside it.

Adding a Starting Message

Now our game has an ending. But to *really* make it complete, let's put something at the beginning, too. We'll add a little message to let the player know what they should be doing, which is chowing down on those berries!

Under **Looks**, you'll find blocks that let our sprites say things in tiny word bubbles. Use one to give the player an introductory message when the flag is first clicked.

Adding a starting message

Again, because of timing, we'll put this message in its own stack. If it was in the same stack as the main loop, the main loop wouldn't start until the word bubble disappeared. The bug would just freeze until the message was gone instead of talking and moving at the same time, like a real hungry bug would.

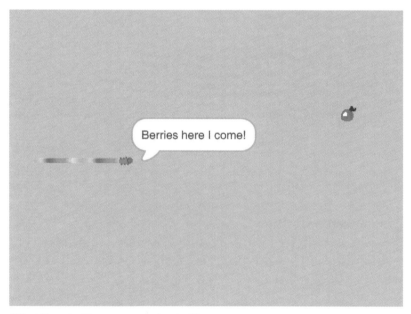

What the starting message looks like

Optional Things to Try

Here are some ideas for additional modifications to *Weird Bug Chowdown* if you want a challenge. All of them can be done using the skills you've learned so far. If you need a hint, open my version of the game in your web browser and click **See inside** to see the game's inner workings. Click **Remix** to create and save your own copy that you can tinker with.

Exercise 1: Animate the berries, and poops' appearances and disappearances.

Instead of suddenly appearing and disappearing, objects can appear gradually, shrink out of sight, or fade away. Instead of using costumes, try graphical effects, like the ghost effect or size changing. You could make a berry look like it's warping in by having it start a few sizes larger than usual and then using a repeat block to make it smaller until it's the normal size. (Recall that a sprite's original size is always 100 percent.) A poop could disappear by shrinking until it's gone. Be creative!

Exercise 2: Show a message the first time the bug eats a bad berry, warning the player about them.

Add a message like "Yuck! Green berries have gone bad!" The trick is to have the message appear *only the first time* the bug eats a bad berry. Make sure the warning only happens on a bad berry, not on a poop! For style, you want the word balloon to come from the bug, not from the berry. You'll probably want to use a variable to track whether the message has appeared yet and a broadcast message to tell the bug to produce the word balloon.

What You Learned

In this chapter, we covered some more advanced ideas. You learned how to make your own variables to keep track of stuff. You programmed your sprites to clone themselves so you could have multiple copies of the same sprite. By broadcasting messages, you gave sprites a way to communicate with each other. You also learned about time pressure and how to use it to make a game more exciting.

In the next chapter, we'll talk about how to make larger games in Scratch, games with multiple levels and scenes. We'll explore what those levels could look like.

Scratch is a great way to learn how to program. The more you learn about Scratch, the more prepared you'll be for a "Serious Adult" programming language. But the basic ideas are the same. If you're just interested in making cool games, Scratch is an excellent choice for doing that. Now let's make some more neat Scratch games. See you in Chapter 3!

3

Hatlight: A Cave Exploring Platform Game

In this chapter, you'll combine everything you learned about programming, character design and animation, and level design to make your own platform game in Scratch. A *platform game* is a fancy name for games like *Super Mario Bros.*, where the player has a cutaway view of the game world and gets around mostly by jumping on platforms suspended in midair, as you can see here.

The platform game we'll create

If you don't want to worry about the programming, go to *http://tinyurl.com/hatlightempty/* to find a version of the game with the platform engine code already written. All it needs is your level design.

About Hatlight

Let's preview a finished version of the *Hatlight* game to give you an idea of what we're making. In this game, you'll be an explorer who uses a hatlight (a flashlight mounted on a hat) to investigate a big, winding cave. Because it's dark underground, you'll need to use your trusty hatlight to find your way around, as shown in the following figure. If you can find some batteries, you can make your light stronger.

Play the game at the following link: *https://scratch.mit.edu/projects/122190314/*. You can use the left and right arrow keys to move around, and the up arrow key to jump. (You can also use the spacebar to jump or even the Z key—whichever feels more natural for you!)

There are seven batteries in all! How many can you find?

Using the hatlight to explore!

Coding Platform Movement

When you're making a game like *Hatlight*, you want to think about how the player will move. The player interacts with your game world by moving, so we want to make moving around the platform feel natural.

Platform movement is a big project, so let's break it down into smaller parts. Breaking down a large task into smaller parts is called *decomposition*. We'll program four types of movement:

- Walking side to side.
- Jumping around (of course!).
- Falling when there's nothing to stand on.
- Climbing sloped or uneven surfaces. (This means we can draw our own levels and not worry about having flat and straight floors. Our game will take place in a cave, so we want a *lot* of bumpy floors.)

If we work on one part at a time, it will be easier to create the game.

Creating a Hitbox Sprite

Let's start by creating a sprite that contains code for all of the player's platforming action.

Create a new project in Scratch and open the Paint Editor. Use the **Rectangle** tool to make a smooth, perfect rectangle, like this.

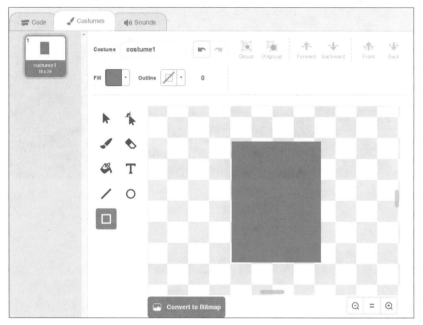

Drawing a hitbox rectangle

Don't make the hitbox too big! We need to leave enough room on the screen so that the player can jump around and explore. When the player is running, jumping, and bouncing around from one platform to another, we'll need to check for *collisions*. A collision lets us know whether the player runs into a wall. If that happens, we can say, "Hey! You and the wall shouldn't be in the same place." Then we can move the player outside the wall.

> **NOTE:** In the next chapter, we'll create another sprite that handles the player's animation. This sprite will move with the hitbox and change costumes depending on the status of the hitbox. For now, the hitbox looks perfectly flat and rectangular for the purpose of making collision easier.

When Scratch checks whether two sprites are touching, the *exact shape* of the sprite matters. For example, if the player sprite has a very long nose, they could hang from a platform by the tip of their nose!

To prevent such situations, we'll make sure Scratch always checks for collisions by making our sprite look like a neat, flat rectangle. This shape is sometimes called a *hitbox* or *bounding box*. In the finished game, it will be invisible. We'll add better animation for the main character later.

Make sure your hitbox is centered on the +. Name the sprite Hitbox.

Drawing a Test Area

Before we code our Hitbox sprite, let's create a test area where we can try out our movement and make sure it works the way we want it to.

Create a sprite named Walls that will contain all the solid objects in our game: the walls, the floor, and the ceilings. The following figure shows all the objects we want the player to collide with.

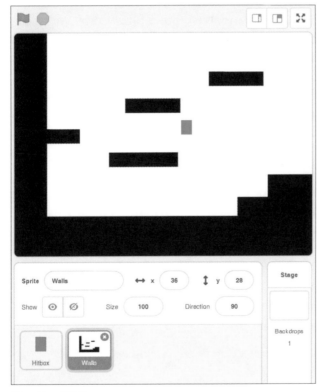

Creating Walls

The full size of the sprite drawing window is the same size as Scratch's game window, so you can draw objects all the way to the edges. As you can see, this example shows the test level. We use the Rectangle tool to draw straight lines for all the floors. Later in this chapter, when we add code to make the player climb over bumpy floors, we'll make the floors look less regular. For now, it's okay to keep them simple.

Make sure your Walls sprite is positioned exactly within the game screen. Here's a handy trick for doing this: give the Walls sprite the code block go to x: 0 y: 0. Then double-click the code block to snap the sprite into position in the middle of the screen. (You can delete the code block afterward.)

We'll put all our levels into the Walls sprite as different costumes later on. But for now, all we need are some walls and platforms for our player to run around in.

Organizing Our Code with Events

Our platform game will involve quite a bit of code. We've already identified four different types of movement we need to code. If we don't decide how to organize the code before we write it, it will get *very* confusing to keep track of.

Fortunately, we already identified different parts of the code that we need: walking, jumping, falling, and climbing. So instead of creating one long stack, we'll create small stacks for each part.

Creating a Chain of Events

Every stack needs to begin with an event, so we'll make a different event for each stack we want. Recall that in Scratch a sprite can receive the messages it broadcasts. This means that we can end each stack by broadcasting the next message in the sequence, creating the equivalent of a forever loop. The last event will call back to the first one, and the code will keep repeating.

Create these events in the Hitbox sprite.

NOTE: The wrap event is for moving from screen to screen. We'll come back to that later!

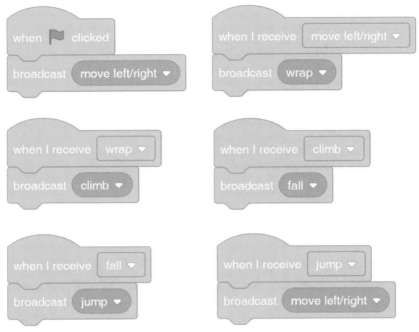

Creating a sequence of events

Now we have a series of events that play out in order, broadcasting the next one in sequence and eventually looping back to the start. None of the events have code in them yet, but we have a basic, working structure to build our game.

Let's explore each event in more detail.

Creating Variables

We'll begin by defining some variables using the Variables tab. We'll put our variables in the when green flag clicked event, before our actual loop starts, as shown next. We only want them to be set once at the beginning of the game.

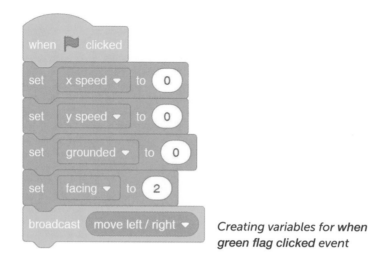

Creating variables for when green flag clicked event

The grounded variable is a special type of variable called a *Boolean* variable, which has one of two values, like true or false, on or off, and so on. In this case, grounded is always either 0 or 1. If it's 0, the player is in midair. If it's 1, the player is on the ground. We can use this value to make sure the player is on the ground before they can jump.

Similar to the way we define variables in programming, we'll set these four variables to the values we want them to start the game at. Each time the game starts, the program will reset all four of these variables.

Coding Player Movement

Now that we've defined our variables and set their default values, we can start programming each stack.

Moving Left and Right

The first stack we'll code is the move left/right stack. The full stack should look something like this.

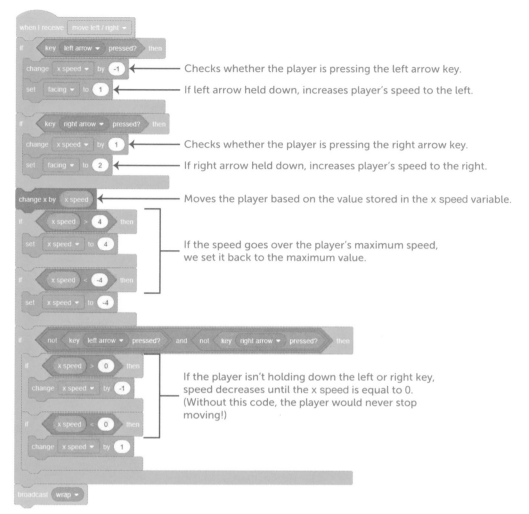

Checks whether the player is pressing the left arrow key.

If left arrow held down, increases player's speed to the left.

Checks whether the player is pressing the right arrow key.

If right arrow held down, increases player's speed to the right.

Moves the player based on the value stored in the x speed variable.

If the speed goes over the player's maximum speed, we set it back to the maximum value.

If the player isn't holding down the left or right key, speed decreases until the x speed is equal to 0. (Without this code, the player would never stop moving!)

The move code

Now let's look at how this stack works step by step. Note that a positive value means the player moves to the right, and a negative value means the player moves to the left, like in a number line.

Climbing Slopes and Steps

So far we've programmed how the player should move on a flat surface. But we haven't yet programmed how they should deal with sloping floors or steps.

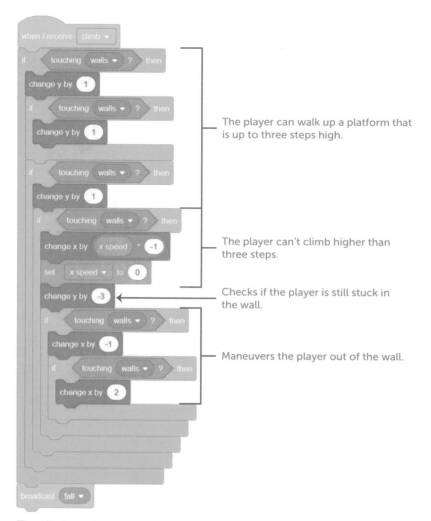

The player can walk up a platform that is up to three steps high.

The player can't climb higher than three steps.

Checks if the player is still stuck in the wall.

Maneuvers the player out of the wall.

The climb code

Let's program players to climb slopes and steps as long as they're not too steep or high. The player can only walk up bumps or slopes that are less than three steps high. If the player takes more than three steps, it will mean the slope is too steep or they've bumped into a wall. So if the player walks into a slope or step that is too high to climb, we'll make it impossible for the player to climb over it. Here's the complete climb code.

This last if () then block to shake the player loose is an emergency measure just to make sure they can never get stuck in the wall!

Falling

Here's the fall code that determines how the player should fall when they're not touching the ground.

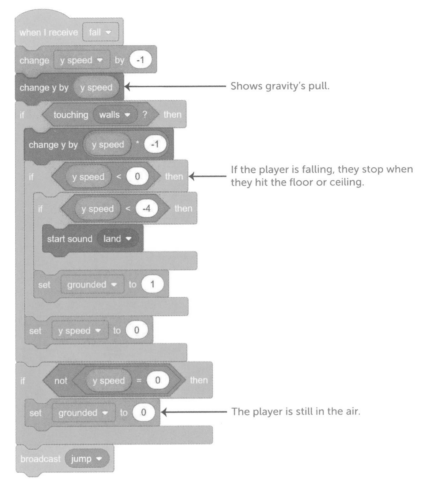

```
when I receive  fall ▼

change  y speed ▼  by  -1

change y by  y speed                          ◄——————————  Shows gravity's pull.

if        touching   walls ▼  ?      then

    change y by  y speed  *  -1

    if        y speed  <  0      then         ◄——————————  If the player is falling, they stop when
                                                            they hit the floor or ceiling.
        if        y speed  <  -4      then

            start sound   land ▼

        set   grounded ▼  to  1

    set   y speed ▼  to  0

if      not    y speed  =  0      then

    set   grounded ▼  to  0                   ◄——————————  The player is still in the air.

broadcast   jump ▼
```

The fall code

Remember that negative numbers mean down and positive numbers mean up. Because of the player's y speed, they won't line up with the floor exactly but might overlap it a bit. If so, we undo their last move by multiplying y speed by –1, causing the player to move in reverse.

If y speed is negative, it means the player bumped into the floor while falling. If it's positive, they've hit the ceiling while jumping. Either way, we set their y speed to 0 because they stop falling.

Jumping

Next, we'll look at how to program the player's jumping motion. Here's the code for jump.

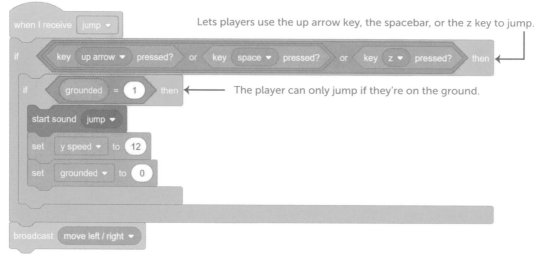

Lets players use the up arrow key, the spacebar, or the z key to jump.

The player can only jump if they're on the ground.

The jump code

Creating Natural Movement with Variables

Why do we use x speed and y speed variables instead of just changing x and y? For example, to set the player's speed to 10, we *could* just increase the player's x by 10 whenever the player presses the right arrow key.

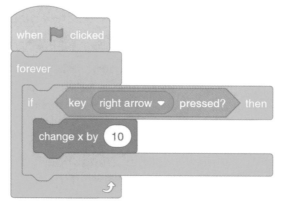

Increasing speed without using variables

In this example, the player has either stopped (speed 0) or is moving (speed 10). The program doesn't allow for any speed in between. This results in a binary movement that looks unnatural.

Binary movement

But if we gradually increase the player's speed over a series of moves, we create a more natural-feeling movement that allows the player to start slow and accelerate to full speed.

Gradual acceleration

Similarly, we can also have the player decelerate instead of stopping instantly.

Deceleration

If you haven't yet, try out your code in your test level. Make sure you change the broadcast wrap block to broadcast climb because we haven't written the wrap part yet. Make changes to the test level by adding a sloped floor. If the player can't jump high enough to reach a platform, make the platform lower. Or change the initial speed of the player's jump. (It's set to 12, as you can see in the jump code.)

You can change how the game feels by experimenting with the numbers in your code blocks. For example, try changing the gravity value or the player's jump speed, the player's maximum walking speed, or the speed of acceleration. Can you make it feel like the player is on the moon? Can you make the player's movement feel really heavy? If you're feeling very confident, try coding a double jump!

Creating a World that's Fun to Explore

Platform games are neat because they give us an interesting way to think about space. In real life, down is always below, and up is always above. Because of gravity, it's usually easier to move downward than upward. That means that getting to higher places can be tricky and require more effort.

But in our exploration platform game, the player can explore the world however they want, with fewer restrictions. It does mean we have to think about space a little differently. We have to consider how different parts of the platform connect with each other.

To really let the player feel like they're exploring, we'll need to create a world that's larger than a single screen, but it will be consistent. For example, if the player walks off the right side of one screen, they should be able to return to where they started by walking left back into the screen. That way, the player can develop a feel for where all the different parts of the world are and how they connect.

Have you ever felt excited to discover a new way to get to a place that you didn't know before? In that moment, you understand your neighborhood a little better: things start to connect like pieces in a puzzle! We can create this feeling in our players by making an interesting world to explore.

Using a Variable to Create a Grid Map

Just like blocks in your neighborhood, we'll arrange our screens into a grid. We'll start with a grid of 4 rooms by 4 rooms, 16 total! Not too big but not too small. We'll number each room to keep track of them, like this.

1	2	3	4
5	6	7	8
9	10	11	12
13	14	15	16

Think of the grid like panels on a comic book page. Looking at this grid, we can easily figure out how to get from one screen to another. To move right one screen, we just add 1 to the number. Room 1 + 1 = room 2. To move left, we subtract 1. To move up or down, we have to get to a different row. For example, if we were trying to move down from room 2 to room 6, we would need to add 4. To go back up, we would subtract 4.

Moving up or down a row requires adding or subtracting 4 because each row has 4 spaces. But in a 5 × 5 grid, we'd need to add 5 to drop down a row!

This kind of movement is sometimes called *flickscreen* because instead of scrolling gradually, the screen flicks to a new image, like turning a page in a book.

We'll use a variable to keep track of which screen the player is on.

Moving from Screen to Screen

We'll use our Walls sprite to store all our screens. It has a costume for each room and changes costumes whenever the player walks off one screen to another. First, let's code moving from one screen to another using the following code.

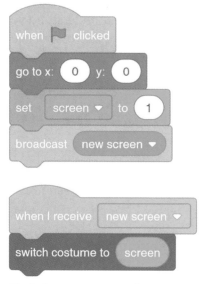

Code for screen swapping

You can see we use a new variable, screen, and a new event, new screen. When the game starts, the Walls sprite sets the screen variable to 1 and then broadcasts the new screen event, changing its costume to match the screen the player is on. From now on, it's mostly the player sprite that will change the screen.

Testing Screen Switching

Now add 15 new costumes to the Walls sprite for a total of 16. It's okay to leave these blank for now, and it's fine if you just name them costume2, costume3, and so on. In fact, it's better to use numbers in their names. Just make sure the numbers are accurate and in the correct order!

The one costume we should fill out is costume2 so we can test whether screen switching works. It doesn't matter what this screen looks like, but try to get platforms along the edge to line up with platforms in the first screen. The easiest way to do this is to use the Select tool to highlight just the edge of the previous screen before copying and pasting it into the new screen.

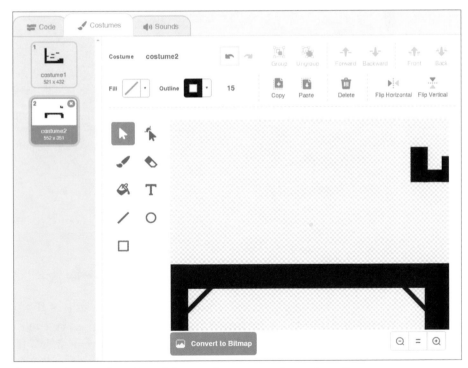

Copy and paste the edge of the previous screen to costume2.

Coding Screen Change

We added a wrap section to our code between the move left/right stack and the climb stack, but we left it blank. Now let's fill it in!

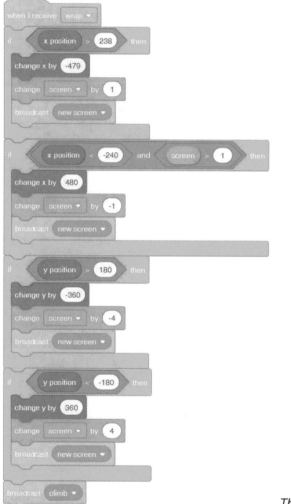

The wrap code

We want the player to be able to walk off the side of the screen and then appear in the next one. For example, if they leave the right side of screen 1, they should appear at the left side of screen 2. We'll write code for all four directions the player can move in: up, down, left, and right.

For each direction, we need to do the following:

1. **Check whether the player is outside the edge of the screen:** Remember that x runs from –240 on the left to 240 on the right, and y runs from 180 at the top to –180 at the bottom.

2. **Move the player to enter the opposite edge of the screen:** When the player exits the bottom of one screen, they should move to the top of the next screen.

3. **Adjust the screen variable:** When moving up and down, the player needs to go –4 or 4 screens at a time.

4. **Broadcast the new screen event:** This lets all the other sprites know the screen has changed, so the Walls sprite will change to the costume that matches the current screen number.

You might need to adjust the values of the x and y positions depending on the size of your Hitbox sprite. Scratch stops sprites before they can get too far off-screen, which means a larger sprite might not be able to reach an x position of –240. In that case, you might try –239 instead. Keep adjusting values until the code works the way you want.

Using Light and Darkness

To make the feeling of exploration stronger, we'll limit what the player can see to the circle of light coming from their hatlight. This is a very simple effect. All the walls and platforms are black. When we put a black background behind them, we can't see where the walls are. By putting a small field of light between the black background and the black walls, we create an area around the player where they can see the walls.

Of course, this only works if all the walls and the background are the same color. If the walls were a different color than the background, the player would see everything, and there would be less mystery and not much to explore in the game. You can use other colors to draw walls if you want them to show up, such as glowing moss on cave walls, or lava cracks.

Creating a field of light between the background and wall

Create a new sprite to represent the beam of light using the **Ellipse**
tool. You can call the sprite Flashlight. An *ellipse* is a roundish shape that
can be wider in one direction than the other, like a football. To draw a
perfect circle, hold down the SHIFT key while you draw it.

Drawing a circle of light

The circle can be any size for now. Later, we'll add code to make it
bigger or smaller depending on the strength of the hatlight's battery life!
Just make sure the center of the circle is over the +. Here, we made it a
bit yellow, like the color of a flashlight.

Make sure the Flashlight sprite is between the black background and the walls. An easy way to adjust where sprites are is to drag a go backward 1 layer block into the Flashlight Scripts tab. You don't have to connect it to an event. When you double-click on a code block, it will run instantly. Just double-click the go backward 1 layer block until the sprite is in the right place. Then you can delete the block.

Coding the Flashlight

Now it's time to code the Flashlight. The following is the entire code that programs how the light will appear.

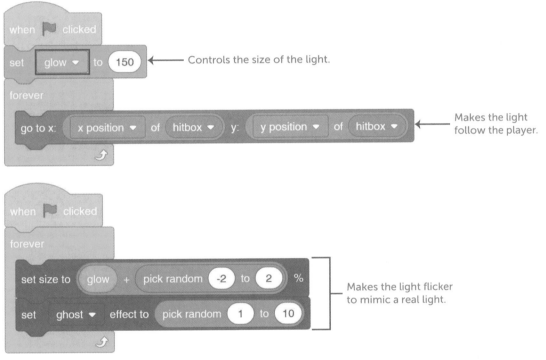

The Flashlight code

Creating Objects to Collect

In Chapter 2, we talked about how collecting berries encouraged the player to think and pay attention to the way the bug moved. In this game, collecting objects can encourage the player to explore and find new paths and secrets in the game environment.

Let's create a sprite for a collectible battery that the player uses to make their hatlight stronger. (That's not how flashlights work in real life, but let's imagine that's how it works!)

*Creating the **battery** sprite*

The batteries should be visible even if they're not in the player's field of light, as long as they're on the same screen. That way, the player can see a battery somewhere onscreen and try to find a way to reach it.

The finished game will have seven batteries the player can collect. To create multiple batteries, we'll use cloning, just like we did to create multiple berries in Chapter 2.

When the game starts, the battery sprite visits every spot a battery should appear, sets its location variable to the correct screen, and clones itself. At the start of a game, the battery creates seven clones, each with a different x and y position and screen number. Each clone uses the location variable to keep track of which screen it should appear on.

After it's finished making clones, the original battery sprite sets its own location to 0, so it doesn't appear on any of the 16 screens. If we don't do this, the parent battery will show up onscreen even though the player can never collect it.

To make sure batteries only appear when the player's on their screens, we use the global screen variable to check whether it matches its local location variable. If it is, it's the correct screen and the clone appears! Otherwise, it disappears.

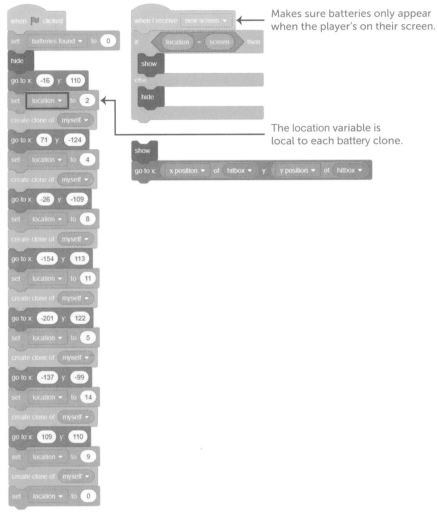

Makes sure batteries only appear when the player's on their screen.

The location variable is local to each battery clone.

The Battery code

If a player makes contact with a battery, we add a value to the global batteries found variable, which was set to 0 at the start of the game, and makes the flashlight's glow variable a little bigger. The more batteries the player collects, the more they can see, helping them track down even more batteries!

What You Learned

In this chapter, we tackled a lot of complex ideas. You learned how to program platform movement and create a character who can walk, climb, jump, and fall. You created a flashlight that the player uses to see in the darkness. By using flickscreen movement, you also created a larger world for your character to explore.

In the next chapter, we'll continue designing *Hatlight* by filling it with secrets, challenges, and more interesting places for the player to discover. We'll also create and animate a player character to replace that hitbox. Take a break, eat a snack, pet a cat, and meet me in Chapter 4 when you're ready!

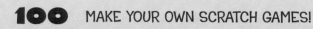

4

Designing Levels

In this chapter, we'll continue with the *Hatlight* game to talk about *level design*, or the design of the different areas in your game. You can use level design to tell stories or let a player know what's important. Level design helps you develop those ideas and mix them up to create the unexpected. In addition, level design can surprise the player or make them experience different feelings: smart, excited, scared, frustrated, or curious.

As a level designer, you need to consider several different concepts at the same time:

A level is a series of challenges or obstacles: How does the player get from one place to another? Do they learn about the game while they figure out how to do so?

A level is a virtual space: How does the level make the player feel? If the level was a real place, would it feel open or cramped? tidy or messy?

A level is an image: The player sees each level as an image on their screen. What does it look like? Is it mostly sharp lines or curves? What part of a level do your eyes notice first?

Considering these elements enables you to tell engaging stories using your levels.

Let's Make Some Levels!

If you skipped programming the game in earlier chapters or just don't want to worry about it, you can find a version of the game with the platform engine code at *http://tinyurl.com/hatlightempty/*.

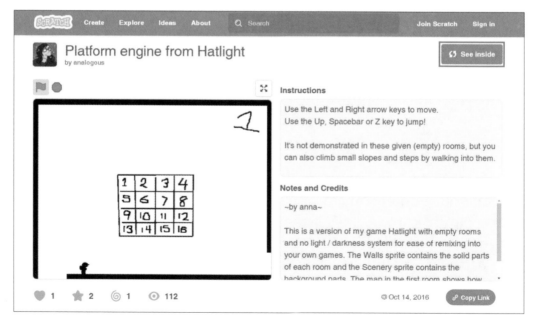

Project page

Just click **See inside** and then click the **File ▶ Save to your computer** to save a copy of the code.

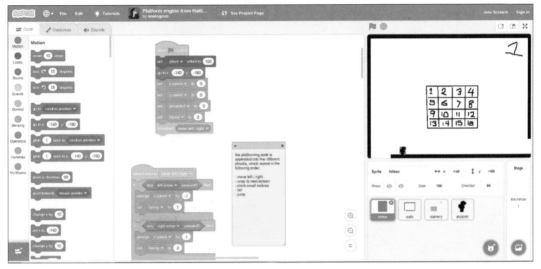

The platform engine code

Now you're ready to make your own levels!

> **NOTE:** Because this version shows the platform engine code, it doesn't have the darkness and flashlight features. If you want them, try tweaking the finished *Hatlight* game instead. You can download it at *https://nostarch.com/scratchgames/*!

Drawing Levels

You can design levels for your game by drawing costumes for the Walls sprite. Each costume should match a room in the grid, as you saw in Chapter 3.

1	2	3	4
5	6	7	8
9	10	11	12
13	14	15	16

If you want your game to have light and darkness, create a second, lighter backdrop that you can use when you're working on levels.

Drawing a Cave

You can use several drawing tools to make different kinds of terrain for your platform. For example, the Brush tool is best for making wiggly, bumpy, and curvy ground, like you would find inside a cave.

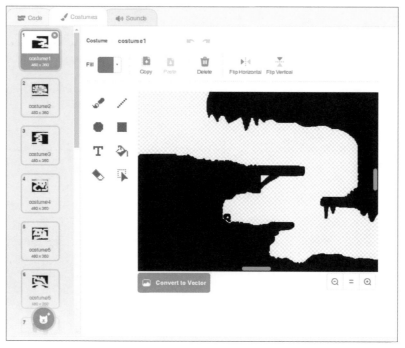

Drawing a cave level

Irregular terrain looks more *natural*, like the hills and ground that you would find in the real world. Things in nature are rarely flat or straight. To make a cool cave or a hill that looks real, try using the Brush tool and your mouse to draw it. (Designers call this *freehand drawing*.) The Line and Rectangle tools make straight lines and are great for drawing objects that look man-made.

Drawing a building

When we build our homes, we usually build them with straight walls and flat floors. In a platform game like *Hatlight*, if the player moves from a bumpy, hilly area into a place full of straight lines, the player will think, "I'm inside a building now."

Note that you can hold down the SHIFT key while drawing a line to make sure it's totally straight. You can also copy and paste parts of a screen using the Select tool to make identical parts.

Saving Details for Later

When you're first drawing levels, try to keep them simple. Don't spend too much time making them look good: start by putting all the platforms in the places you want them. You can come back and add details later.

Rough first draft

Final draft after adding details

Play your levels as you're sketching them. After you make sure they work, only *then* go back and make them look nicer.

Here are some tricks for adding detail to your levels:

 Adjust the pen size for finer detail: Use a smaller brush to add branches to a tree.

 Use the mouse to draw dots: Instead of clicking and dragging, try just clicking to place a single dot. These dots could be pebbles or fallen rubble.

 Draw with the Eraser tool: Use the eraser to draw cracks and holes, and other details.

Now that you've explored ways to add authentic and fun details to your platforms, let's keep going.

Things to Keep in Mind

Keep in mind that the game considers everything you draw in the Walls sprite as a solid object. So, if you're not careful, you can create places the player can stand on that they shouldn't be able to.

The player shouldn't be able to stand on a wall like this!

One way around this problem is to make walls slope away from the player. Another is to use the Line / or Rectangle ☐ tools to make sure your walls are straight. Try making a straight wall and then adding some tiny pockmarks using the Eraser tool ◆.

Sloped wall

Also, check bumpy floors and sloped surfaces to make sure the player can walk across them! The player should be able to climb bumps or slopes 3 pixels tall but will get stuck if a bump is any taller.

A stuck player!

Make sure the floors and platforms line up between screens, or else the player can end up suspended in midair or stuck in the floor when moving from screen to screen. The easiest way to avoid this is to use the Select tool ➤ to highlight the edge of one screen, and then copy and paste it to the adjacent screen, like this.

Copying and pasting one edge of the screen to the next

As mentioned earlier, anything you draw in a costume for the Walls sprite will be solid, even if you try to remove it by drawing over it with the color white. All that white you draw will still be treated as solid ground. (But if you want solid white ground, this is no big deal.)

To get rid of something, you need to use the Eraser tool 🩹.

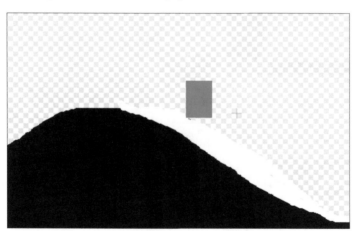

Player on solid white ground

Scratch considers even a single speck of color in the Walls sprite a solid object.

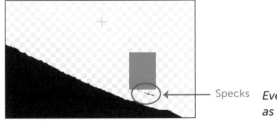

Specks — *Even specks count as solid ground.*

If the player gets stuck somewhere or seems to float in midair, use the Zoom tool ⊕ to check for tiny specks left over from erasing.

Adding Background Scenery

What if we want to add objects to our levels that aren't solid, like a tree in the background or a small dog? No problem!

Background scenery

Let's add a Scenery sprite to add details to the background. Like the Walls sprite, this sprite will have a costume for each room. But unlike the Walls sprite, the items we draw in the Scenery costume won't be solid. Instead, they'll be in the background, so the player can walk in front of them.

If you've uploaded the complete game from the book's site, you should already have a Scenery sprite. Just draw background objects onto the costume that matches the screen you want them to appear on.

> **NOTE:** The costumes have numbers on them to help you keep track of which screen is which. Feel free to erase them when you draw your own backgrounds!

Otherwise, you'll need to program a Scenery sprite, like this.

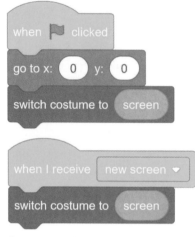

Scenery code

Similar to the new screen event we added to the player that broadcasts whenever the screen changes, the new screen message changes its costume to match the screen we're on after the Scenery sprite receives the message. Be sure to give the Scenery sprite 16 costumes in total!

You want the Scenery sprite to be in front of the Flashlight sprite so the light from the flashlight won't cover it up. You can adjust the depth of sprites using the go to front layer and go backward X layers blocks in the Looks tab. Remember that you can double-click a code block to execute it immediately, even when the game isn't running. When you double-click the go backward –1 layers block, it brings a sprite forward a single layer.

The go backwards –1 layers block

When you're drawing background scenery, make sure the Walls sprite is set to the costume that matches the Scenery sprite. That way you can tell whether the background scenery you're drawing lines up with walls and platforms.

Teaching the Player How to Play

Because *Hatlight* is an exploration game, the player chooses the parts of the game they see in the order they want. But before we give the player any big choices, let's make sure they understand the basics.

We'll start the game with two screens that introduce them to the most important ideas they need to know, such as how they'll move around, how high they can jump, and whether they can see the entire level they're in at once. (Hint: no, they can't.)

First, we want the player to understand how light and darkness work. So the game starts with an opening screen where the player begins outside the cave in full daylight, and then enters the cave where it's dark.

Screen 1: the cave entrance

We use the Scenery sprite to provide the daylight. When the player steps out of the daylight into the darkness, the hatlight appears. This transition makes sure the player *notices* when the hatlight comes on.

As the player climbs down the screen into the cave, a spooky skull appears in the corner. That's just my way of showing the player they can use their light to discover things!

Screen 1: inside the cave

On the second screen, we introduce the next most important idea: the player sees their first battery and understands that it's an object to collect.

Screen 2 shows a battery somewhere nearby

The player enters this screen at the bottom and sees the battery at the top. This is why it's important that the batteries are visible in the darkness. The player can see where it is but can't see how to get to it without exploring their environment. Batteries give them a reason to explore.

In the first screen, the player learns some valuable information about the game. Players learn there are batteries to find and what the batteries look like. Batteries are always visible but sometimes hard to reach. If your players try to reach a battery and touch it at this point, they'll learn they can collect them. (If they skip this step, there are more opportunities to learn this lesson later.)

The simplest areas in a game can teach you a lot of information about the game. When you play other games, pay attention to what the game is sneakily teaching you.

Let's talk about some of the ways level design teaches game play.

Showing Objects Players Can't Reach

On screen 2, the player sees a battery and, if they explore, eventually figures out a way to reach it. That all happens on a single screen. But because our game lets the player move from screen to screen in different directions, we can create even more mysteries for the player to investigate across multiple screens.

After the first two screens, the player enters a big shaft that runs from the top of the map to the bottom, connecting lots of different areas. In the middle of the shaft, they might discover this battery.

It's so close yet so far! The way to it is blocked by a cave-in. There's no obvious way to get to it on this screen. To get to it, the player needs to approach it from a different direction.

A cave-in blocks the path to a battery.

They need to first go up and around through another screen, and then drop into a pit. If they can land on the ledge below, they can reach the battery. Learning the ledge is there, of course, requires either careful exploration or an accidental tumble into the pit.

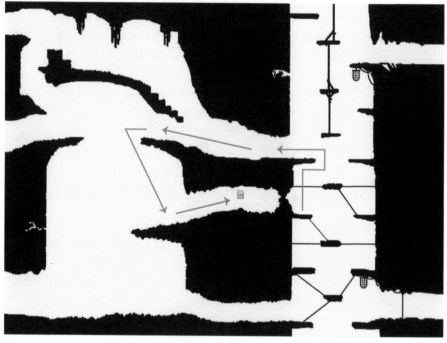

Reaching the battery requires finding a way around.

When you show players something they can't reach, you're giving them a problem to solve. Figuring out how to get to this battery makes the player think about how different screens relate to each other, forcing the player to explore and put that information together to solve the problem. When they finally collect the battery, it feels satisfying: "I figured it out! Take *that*, game."

Creating Interesting Landmarks

A good way to make your levels intriguing and help the player remember where objects are is to create distinct areas. For example, you can turn two screens into a cool crystal zone.

Crystal zone

Here, we use straight lines and sharp angles to create screens that look and feel very different from the rest of the game. Keep in mind that a level is not only a place and a series of challenges and puzzles, but it's also a picture.

These screens look cool, but they should look like they belong together as well, which will link them in the player's brain. When the player is trying to remember what the map looks like, it's easier to remember where a big area made up of two screens is than a single smaller screen. For example, it's easier to find your way to a neighborhood than to a single house.

Also, notice how the passage leading into the crystal zone from the central mine shaft has a few crystals in it, like a signpost pointing the way. "This way to the crystal zone!"

Entrance to the crystal zone

Some other distinct areas in this game are the castle zone and the big mine shaft. The mine shaft is sometimes called a "hub" area. Think of it as the center of a bicycle wheel, where all the different spokes connect to. If the player gets lost anywhere in the cave, they'll eventually find their way back to the mine shaft.

Creating Animation

It would be a waste to build a beautiful world and leave the player looking like a running, jumping red box. Let's create and animate a player character.

> **NOTE:** If you've uploaded the complete game from the book's site, you should see an animated player sprite. Feel free to edit, change, or redraw any of the animations.

The Hitbox sprite does the moving, jumping, and bumping into walls. All of the movement code is in that sprite. In this section, we'll create a *second* sprite to handle all the animation and attach it to the same Hitbox. When we make the Hitbox invisible, the player should only see our cool animations.

Create a new sprite called Explorer, which will be the animation sprite. Its costumes will hold the character's animation, and we'll write code to tell it when to show each animation.

Animating the Player's Movements

Animation communicates how the character is moving. In *Hatlight*, the player performs the following movements:

- Standing still
- Walking
- Jumping
- Falling

Although standing still isn't really a movement, we need to communicate when the player is *not* moving, too. If the player looked the same walking as they did standing still, you wouldn't be able to tell the difference between the two. So we want it to have its own appearance.

Standing Still

The first costume is the standing still pose. It should be centered on the + and be about the same size as the Hitbox. A good idea is to copy the Hitbox costume and paste it into this costume to use as a guide. When you're done drawing, you can delete any remaining parts of the original Hitbox costume.

Standing costume

Mine faces toward the right. For now, let's draw all the costumes so they face toward the right. Later, we'll use the **Select** tool to flip them around and make left-facing versions.

Walking

Right-click your standing still costume and select **duplicate**. Using your standing pose as a starting point, change the new costume so it looks like your character is in midstride.

Walking animation

This is the simplest kind of walking animation. In one frame, the character's legs are together, and in the next, they're apart. When we alternate between the two costumes, it'll look like the character is walking. In real life, walking is much more complicated, but for our game, this is fine.

> **NOTE:** Try looking up a slow-motion video of someone walking sometime!

When you look closely at the grid lines in the walking animation frames, you'll see that the head in the frame on the right is a bit lower. This adds a little *bobble* that makes the walking motion more believable. As the player walks, their head bobbles up and down with the rhythm of walking.

Jumping

For jumping, duplicate your standing costume again as a starting point.

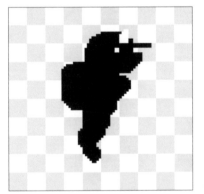

Jumping costume

Jumping is supposed to communicate upward motion (also known as *upness*), so here we raise the head even higher and make the character's eyes face upward. We also tilt their feet like they're springing off the ground to emphasize the vertical movement of jumping.

Falling

For falling, we move the head lower and position the head super low too.

Falling costume

When the player reaches the peak of a jump, we'll switch from the jumping costume to the falling costume, so everything about the falling pose should communicate downward motion (also known as *downness*). The legs and feet are bracing for a landing.

Or You Can Just Draw a Blob!

Your character can be whatever you like. If animating the human form is too tricky, try making something else. For example, a blob is super easy to animate.

Blob animation

Draw a normal-looking blob, and then make two more costumes: a taller, thinner blob and a shorter, wider blob. If you alternate between normal, tall, normal, wide, normal, tall, and so on, your blob will appear to squish around as it moves. You can use the Select tool to change your blob's height and width more easily.

You can even make your character look like a snake (snakes are just the letter S) or a weird bug. If you make your bug move slightly up and down between costumes, it'll look like it's scuttling along the ground. Draw whatever you would like!

Creating a Mirror Image of a Costume

So far, you've made a bunch of right-facing animations. Now let's flip them around to create the left-facing versions. That way, your character can face the direction it's walking or jumping in.

Using the Select tool to mirror

Making left-facing costumes is easy. Duplicate a costume, and then draw a box around it using the **Select** tool. In the upper right of the drawing window, click the **Flip Horizontal** button next to the Flip Vertical button to flip the costume. Then make sure it's centered on the + again.

Make a left- and right-facing version of each of your costumes.

Coding the Animations

Animation can be a bit intimidating to code, but it's very simple.

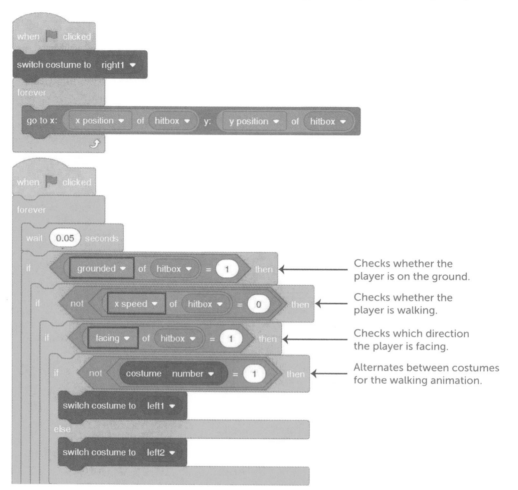

Checks whether the player is on the ground.

Checks whether the player is walking.

Checks which direction the player is facing.

Alternates between costumes for the walking animation.

Animation code

The first stack of code makes sure the Explorer sprite is always at the same place as the Hitbox sprite. As the Hitbox moves around the screen, so will our animations. The second code stack chooses the appropriate costume.

The last thing to do is make sure the Hitbox is invisible now that we have an animated character to display. We can use the ghost effect for that.

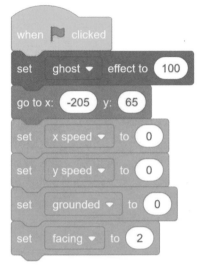

Set ghost effect to 100

This block sets the ghost effect to 100, which means 100 percent invisible.

Now the player character is animated!

You should now see just the character, not the red rectangle that handles all the numbers.

Additional Challenges

Here are some additional touches that can make your game more complete:

Intro: When the game starts, the player sees the game title before their character appears. Can you make a title screen for your game? You'll need to hide all the game sprites until the title screen ends.

Ending: What happens when the player collects all the batteries? How does the story end? Create an ending to the game.

Sound effects: You might want to include some sound effects for important actions, like jumping or collecting a battery. You can use Scratch's built-in sound library, or you can make your own sounds. You'll learn more about sound effects in the next chapter!

What You Learned

In this chapter, you learned about level design and what you can do with it. Level design is about storytelling, and a good storyteller thinks of each level as a set of challenges, an imaginary place, and a picture on a screen all at the same time. You also learned how to animate your character, using motion to communicate important things about a character, like where they're going and how they're getting there.

In Chapter 5, we'll talk about how to add sound and music to your games. It'll be a lot of fun!

5

Creating Sound Effects

Sound and music are ancient and incredible art forms in their own right. I'm sure you have a favorite song! People have been making music and noise for thousands of years, and in this chapter, you'll learn how to do some amazing things with music and sound in your games. So how do games use sound?

Sound effects provide information. How does a player know that they've collected a treasure or gotten chomped by a monster? In *Weird Bug Chowdown* in Chapter 2, whenever the bug touches something, good or bad, the game plays a sound effect. Sound lets the player know something important has taken place. It also shapes how they feel about what's happened. That's why eating a berry produces a hearty "chomp" sound and touching a bad berry or a poop produces an "eww."

Music helps to set the tone. Think of an exciting scene in your favorite movie. What was the music like? Was it fast and energetic? Did it make you feel excited? What about the music in a sad scene? Was it slow and moody? Music affects how we feel about what happens while we're listening to it, and the same is true in games. Many of the games you play probably have light, boppy music that creates a playful mood. Would you feel differently about what was happening in these games if the music was heavy and sad?

Maybe you play an instrument, or maybe you have absolutely no idea how to make music. Well, it's much easier than you'd think to make audio for your games!

Sound Design Tools

In this chapter, you'll learn about a few different programs that you can use to make music and sound. Like all the other tools we've worked with in this book, you can find all of these programs on the internet for free. First, you'll record and edit sounds using a program called Audacity. Second, you'll generate sound effects with sfxr. Third, you'll learn how to compose short music loops using Drum Circle.

You probably won't need to use all of these tools. Most likely, one of them will feel easiest and most appropriate for your particular games. Everyone has their own *practice,* or personal process of making stuff. There's no such thing as the right process.

Recording and Editing Sounds with Audacity

You already have the means to make great game sound effects. I'm talking about your voice as well as pretty much every object around you! In the finished *Hatlight* game, I made the jumping sound effect by saying "Hup!" into my computer's mic. The crunching sound the ground makes as you walk around is me shaking a bunch of dice in front of the mic.

Scratch has a built-in microphone button in the Sounds tab that lets you record your own sounds, but Audacity lets you do more with your recording. For example, you can make sounds fade in and fade out, add special effects, and even cut out the bits you don't like.

Naturally, these tools only work if your computer has a microphone. Most laptops and tablets come with a built-in microphone. If your computer doesn't have one, you can either buy one at your local electronics store (a cheap one is fine!) or start with "Generating Sounds with sfxr" on page 137, where we'll use other tools that don't require a mic. You can find Audacity at *https://sourceforge.net/projects/audacity/*. Download the version appropriate for your computer system, and we'll get started!

Recording a Deadly Plummet

Open Audacity, and you'll see this screen.

Pause   Play   Record

Shows which mics are connected
to your computer

Audacity interface

There's a lot on the screen, but you don't need to worry about most of it. Find the microphone near the bottom of the huge toolbar at the top. The Recording Device menu next to the mic lists every sound device connected to your computer. If you're having trouble recording, try choosing different devices from this list. Audacity might not be using the right one.

The most important buttons on the screen are the big Pause, Play, and Record buttons at the top. Let's record our first sound!

Imagine a game about a cave explorer, like the one in Chapter 4. The explorer is under the earth, walking on a narrow stone bridge over an underground river. With every step she takes, she hears the sound of gravel cracking and shifting. She is stepping slowly and carefully. Finally, she steps on a part of the bridge that is too old and thin, and the bridge breaks underneath her! As she plummets out of sight, her yell trails off: "AAAAAAAAAAaaaaaaaaaaa..." (Don't worry—the river is full of Subterranean Pillowfish. She'll be fine!)

Let's try to re-create that yelling sound. Click the **Record** button and yell "AAAAAAAAAA" into the microphone. Make it a long sound, because it's a long way to the bottom of the cave! Don't worry about making your voice trail off. We'll do that using special effects. Click the **Stop** button when you're done recording. Your screen should look something like this.

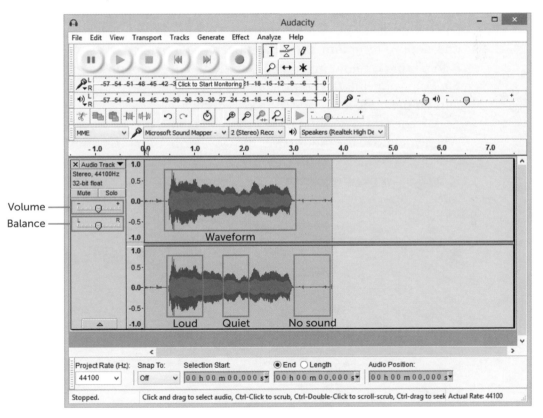

The lumpy blue shape is your recording's waveform. A *waveform* is a picture of what the sound looks like. The highest parts are the loudest sounds. Shorter parts are quieter sounds. You should also see two flat parts at the beginning and end. These are the quiet parts before and after you started making noise.

Before we make changes to the waveform, let's go over a couple sliders (circled in the preceding image).

The top one goes from – to + and controls the volume. If your sound is too quiet or loud, you can adjust it by moving this slider. Below that is a slider that goes from L to R. That controls the *balance* of the sound, whether the sound plays from the left speaker (or headphone) or the right. The slider starts exactly in the middle, which is where you'll usually want it to be.

Sound Selections

When you click **Play**, you'll hear the whole waveform, including the quiet parts at the beginning and end. Depending on when you started and stopped recording, these quiet parts could be long or very short. Before using a sound in a game, you should get rid of any empty spaces. After all, you want the game sound to play exactly when the explorer falls off the bridge, not after a second of silence.

We can edit our sound by selecting different parts of the waveform. When you move the mouse over the waveform, the cursor changes into an "I" shape. You can click and drag to select different parts of the sound. Select just the part with the "aaaaaaaa" sound, none of the flat (silent) parts.

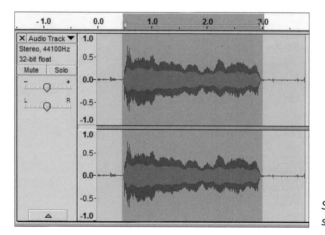

Selecting a part of the sound you want

Try clicking **Play** again. You should hear just the "aaaaaaaa" part. Notice that when you move the cursor to either end of the selection, it becomes a pointing finger. You can click either end of the selection and drag it to change where the selection begins or ends. Try selecting just a part of the waveform, somewhere in the middle. Now when you click **Play**, just the part that's selected will play.

Any edit we make will happen to the part of the waveform we select. So, to get rid of the gap at the beginning of our recording, we first need to select it. Adjust the end of the selection until the entire gap, and nothing else, is selected.

> **NOTE:** If you're worried about whether your selection is in the right place, you can always use the magnifying glass icons to zoom in on the waveform.

Near the top of the window, click **Edit ▶ Delete**. The selected part of the sound should be gone.

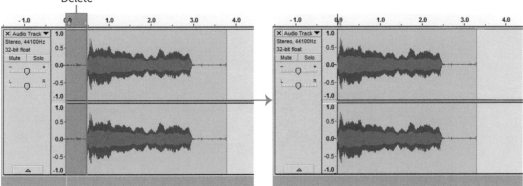

Deleting the sound you don't want

Try selecting and deleting the flat part at the end of the sound too! The part of the sound where you're making noise into the mic should be all that's left. Now, let's use selections to change what our sound effect *sounds* like.

Using Effects Tools

We want our falling sound to be nice and long. How long is yours? Probably not long enough! Remember that it's a very long drop to the bottom of the cave. Fortunately, there's a way to stretch a sound to make it longer.

When you click the **Effects** menu at the top of the screen, you'll see a ridiculous number of different options. Here's a summary of those handiest:

Change Pitch: *Pitch* is how high or low something sounds. Think of pitch in terms of mythological creatures. If you lower your pitch, you'll start to sound like a troll. If you raise your pitch, you'll start to sound like a fairy.

Change Speed: This option lets you change the length of your sound, which is one way to make it longer. But when you change *speed*, you also affect the pitch. If you slow down your sound, the pitch gets lower. If you speed it up, the pitch rises.

Change Tempo: *Tempo* is a music term for the speed of a piece of music. Change Tempo lets you make your sound longer or shorter *without* changing the pitch of your voice.

Let's use Change Tempo to make our recording longer. Click **Effects ▶ Change Tempo**.

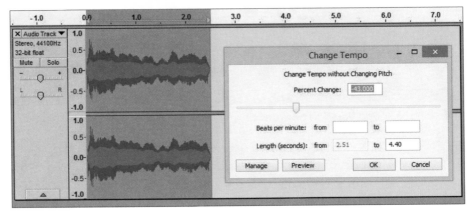

Before tempo change

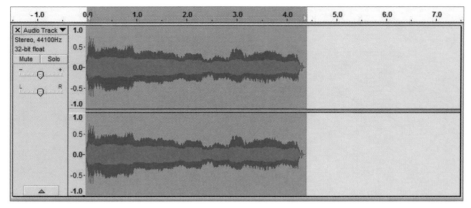

After tempo change

A Change Tempo window should pop up with a bunch of different options, but they're all different ways of doing the same thing. The easiest option to use is the slider. The exact center of the slider is the speed of your sound right now. Move the slider to the right to speed it up. Move it to the left to slow it down. You can move the slider and click **Preview** to test what your sound will sound like.

Lower the tempo and click **OK**. Your waveform should get longer. Now when you play your sound, your voice should sound a little slower!

Now let's make our sound slowly fade out as we plummet out of sight. Use the cursor to select about three-quarters of your sound. We want a bit at the beginning to stay the same.

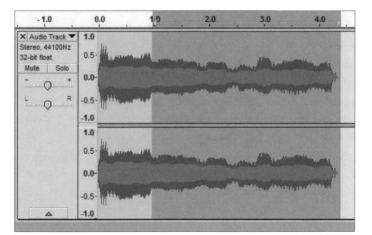

Making your sound fade out

Now click **Effects ▸ Fade Out**.

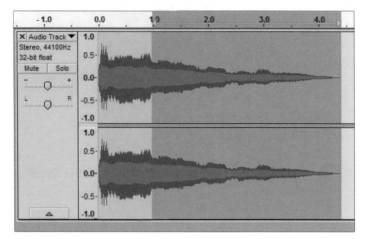

Post fade out

Your waveform has changed shape. It starts wide and then gets smaller and smaller until it reaches a single point at the end. Fade out is a very handy effect that matches itself to the size of your selection. When you fade out a long selection, you'll get a slow, gradual fade. When you fade out a short selection, you'll get a much quicker fade. There's also a Fade In effect that does the same thing but in reverse. The selection starts silent and then gets louder until it reaches normal volume.

Play your new sound! Keep in mind that the Play button will play only what you've selected. To get out of your selection, click the **Rewind** (|<<) button.

Exporting Sounds

One important detail to know about Audacity is that *saving* doesn't mean what it does in other programs. When you click **File ▸ Save Project** in Audacity, you'll save a specific kind of file called a *project* file. Only Audacity can open a project file. It's useful when you're doing complicated sounds, like working with multiple channels of audio. But you can't import an Audacity project file into your Scratch game.

Instead, you'll have to export the audio into a format that Scratch can use by clicking **File ▸ Export Audio**.

You can also highlight a part of the waveform and click **Export Selected Audio** to export just a selection of a recording.

Exporting audio

Audacity can export audio in many different file formats. Usually, you'll want to use *WAV*, which is a sound format that most programs use, Scratch included.

When you export your sound effect, an Edit Metadata window should pop up. If you were working on a podcast or a track from your new EP, you might want to fill out the metadata. But for a video game sound effect, you don't need to worry about metadata. Just click **OK** to export your sound.

Now you can import your sound into your Scratch game. From the Sounds tab, hover over the Choose a Sound icon until the menu comes up. Click the **Choose a New Sound** icon.

Importing my amazing screams

Using Sounds from the Internet

You can make lots of different sound effects by making noises with your mouth or by knocking objects together in front of your microphone. But sometimes you need a very specific sound, like a bird tweeting, that you can't make using the stuff in your house. In these situations, you can use sounds at *https://freesound.org/*.

![The freesound.org homepage showing search results for "bird"]

The freesound.org *homepage*

On the Freesound site, you'll find lots of unique sounds recorded by different people. These sounds are released under the Creative Commons license. You can use them for free as long as you include the name of the sound's creator.

Scratch has a Notes and Credits space on each of your game's pages. That's the perfect place to give a shout-out to those who contributed to your finished game. Just enter something like "Bird call sound recorded by ErgoBirdo on *https://freesound.org/*." That's called *attribution*!

Some sounds will list several different sounds. For example, you might want to use a single bird tweet from a list of 10. Or you might want the sound to be faster or slower, or to fade in or out. That's when you would use Audacity. You can load any sound you download from Freesound, edit it, and export a version to use in your game. Just make sure you always credit the person who recorded the original sound!

Generating Sounds with sfxr

The sfxr tool quickly generates simple video game sound effects. If you've played an older video game, commonly known as "8-bit," you know what sfxr sound effects sound like: "bleeps" and "bloops" and "HHSSHHSSHSSes." You don't need a mic to use sfxr: you just click buttons and slide sliders.

Created by Tomas Pettersson, sfxr can be found on his website at *http://tinyurl.com/getsfxr/*. The sfxr tool is made for Windows computers, but if you have a Mac, a link on that site leads to cfxr, a Mac version of the program.

Run sfxr, and you'll see this.

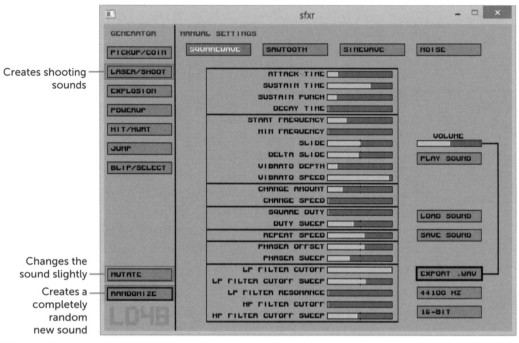

Creates shooting sounds —

Changes the sound slightly —

Creates a completely random new sound —

The sfxr interface

Don't worry about the sliders for now! We'll look at the buttons first. On the left is a bunch of Generator buttons, such as Laser/Shoot, Explosion, Powerup, and so on. Click the **Laser/Shoot** button a few times, and sfxr creates a number of different shooty sounds for you.

Experiment with the generators until you find a sound you like. Click the **Play Sound** button to hear your sound again. Then try clicking the **Mutate** button (at the bottom left) to change the sound. Each time you click Mutate, the sound changes a little. Notice how the sliders change as the sound changes.

The sfxr program only remembers the last sound it generated. So if you find one you really love, be sure to save it before you make a new one! We'll talk more about saving and exporting sounds in a moment.

Waveforms

Four buttons are across the top of the sfxr window: Squarewave, Sawtooth, Sinewave, and Noise. One of them should be highlighted right now. You can use these four different kinds of waveforms to create sound effects.

Try switching between the buttons and clicking **Play Sound** to hear how a sound differs in each waveform. Here is what each waveform looks like.

Squarewave gets its name from its blocky waveform when you look at it up close. Squarewaves are clear and chunky. Most of the sounds you make in sfxr will probably be squarewaves.

Squarewave

Sawtooth is pointy when looked at up close, like the teeth of a saw. This waveform sounds tinnier and grittier than squarewaves, which is ideal when you want to use a more metallic sound effect.

Sawtooth

Sinewave is a smooth up-and-down curve that sounds spacey and bubbly. When you want sound effects for space crystals bouncing around on an ice planet, sinewaves will work well.

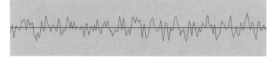

Sinewave

Noise looks like a scribble you might draw in your notebook. It's all over the place, so it sounds crashy and, well, noisy. Noise is perfect for explosions and the sound of ocean waves.

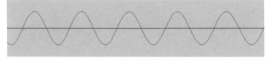

Noise

Other generator buttons produce different waveforms. Pickup/Coin produces a squarewave, and Explosion produces noise. When you find a sound you like, listen to how it sounds using each waveform.

Changing Sounds Using Sliders

What if you want your sound to be longer or *weirder*? By playing with sfxr's many sliders, you can make all sorts of changes to your sound.

The best way to get a sense of what each slider does is to generate a sound and then play with the sliders to hear how the sound changes. Here are some of the most useful sliders.

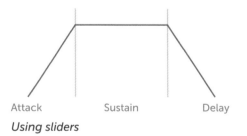

Attack   Sustain   Delay

Using sliders

Attack, Sustain, and Decay

Sometimes you'll want your sound to be a different length or to slowly fade out. The Attack, Sustain, and Decay tools affect your sound's timing. Sound nerds refer to this as the sound's *envelope*, because it's how your sound will be delivered. Here are the effects of each tool:

Attack Time is the amount of time it takes your sound to fade in. Set it low for an instant sound or high for a long buildup.

Sustain Time is the middle of the sound, which is after it has faded all the way in and before it starts to fade out. When you just want your sound to be longer, give it a higher Sustain Time.

Decay Time is the fade-out. A high Decay Time slowly fades to silence. A low Decay Time just cuts out the sound.

Slide, Vibrato, and Change

Slide, Vibrato, and Change give your sound more depth. If you can't hear the change, lengthen your sound's Sustain Time. Here are the effects of each tool:

Slide makes your sound slide up or down, depending on whether it's higher or lower than the center. The Slide Delta slider specifies how fast it raises or lowers, either quickly or slowly.

Vibrato adds a cool oscillating effect to your sound. It's kind of wiggly. The Vibrato Depth slider specifies how wiggly the vibrato gets, and the Vibrato Speed specifies how fast it goes. At a low speed, you can easily hear it move up and down. At a high speed, the oscillations blend together into a buzzier sound.

Change lets you change how high or low the middle of your sound is. Slide changes the sound gradually, but Change does it instantly. You can use Change to make your sound seem like it has multiple notes. Change Amount specifies how high or low the sound should become: to the right is higher, and to the left is lower. Change Speed specifies where in the sound the change happens. A higher Change Speed happens almost immediately, and a lower Change Speed happens later in the sound.

Exporting Sounds

As with Audacity, *saving* a sound and *exporting* it in sfxr are two different processes. Clicking **Save Sound** produces a file that only works with sfxr. The file keeps track of all your slider settings, so if you want to make changes later, you must save your sound.

Clicking **Export .Wav** produces a *WAV* file that most game-making tools (like Scratch) can read. But sfxr can't read *WAV* files. So if you don't save your sound before you export it and want to make changes to your sound later, *tough noogies*.

Obviously, the best practice is to save your sound *and* export a *WAV* file for your game. That way, if you decide to make it shorter, longer, or weirder, you can reload your sound file in sfxr. Then you can export a *WAV* file of your new sound.

The bfxr Tool

If you're comfortable using sfxr, you might want to try the more complicated bfxr.

The bxfr interface

Created by Stephen Lavelle, bfxr is somewhat of a sequel to sfxr. It has more waveforms, more options, and more features in general. One useful bfxr feature is that it keeps track of all the new sounds you create using the Generator and Randomize buttons. So if you want to go back to a sound you generated earlier, you can. You probably won't need most of the new options in bfxr unless sfxr doesn't provide enough features for the sounds you want to create. You can download the tool at *https://www.bfxr.net/*.

Creating Music Loops with Drumcircle

Most music you listen to has a beginning and an end, and your favorite summer jam is probably only a couple of minutes long. In games, it's often impossible to tell how long a song needs to play. Each player takes a different amount of time to finish the game. Some will finish very quickly, and others will spend a long time exploring.

That's why most game music is written to be looped. It doesn't have an end. Instead, it wraps back around to the beginning and keeps going. That way, the song can fit however long the player ends up playing the game.

We'll use the Drumcircle program to make short music loops. Created by Andi McClure, Drumcircle is simple and fun to use. You can download it at *http://tinyurl.com/getdrumcircle/*.

When you run it, you'll see a very simple menu. Click the **Play** button to get started. You'll see a screen that looks like this.

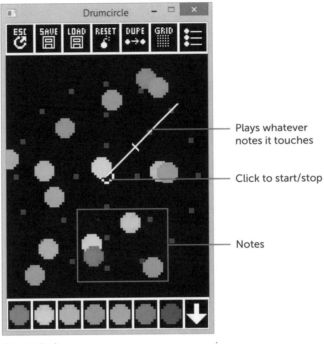

Plays whatever notes it touches

Click to start/stop

Notes

Drumcircle

Your screen won't look exactly the same as the one you see here. When you start Drumcircle, it'll create a loop from random notes. Drumcircle works similar to an old submarine radar screen. (Maybe you've seen one in a movie.) As the line (or *sweep* in radar parlance) moves around the circle, it plays the notes that it touches. By placing notes in the circle, you decide which notes are played.

Play with the program a bit to get a feel for it! You can drag notes around to move them, or drag new notes from the bottom to add them. Click a note to hear what it sounds like. When you click the arrow at the bottom right, you can cycle through even more notes, drum sounds, and effects. Also, you can start and stop the sweep by clicking the center of the circle.

Making a Drum Loop

All right, let's make a simple drum loop. Click the **Reset** button at the top to clear all the notes. You should be left with a bunch of dots.

Clears all the notes

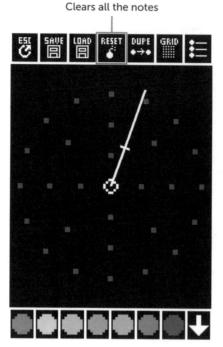

A blank slate

Around the outside of the circle are 16 dots, which make Drumcircle a *16-step sequencer*. A sequencer makes music by putting notes in a sequence, and 16 step refers to the 16 notes the sequencer uses. Electronic music-making tools use 16 step as a common format.

The second circle inside the biggest circle has 8 spots (half of 16), and the innermost circle has 4 spots (a quarter of 16 and half of 8). These inner spots are guidelines that will help us make our loop. If we play a note 16 times in the outer circle, it produces a very fast beat. If we play a note 8 times in the second circle, it'll be slower, playing it half as often. Playing a note 4 times in the inner circle is slowest of all.

Adding Some Drums

Let's make a simple loop. We'll start by adding some drums to create a rhythm. A drum rhythm is often the backbone of a music piece. It gives the rest of the instruments a structure to build from. This simple drum line will be our structure.

When you click the colored circles at the bottom of the screen, they get higher in pitch from left to right. These are musical notes and are usually lettered A to G. We'll come back to this later. To start, we want a drum line, so click the arrow until you see the drum icons.

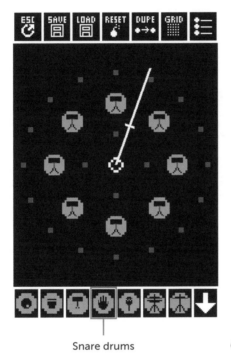

Snare drums

Creating a drum line

Try clicking some of the drums to hear what they sound like. There are lots of different drum sounds, including a hand clap. For our drum line, we'll use the snare drum, which looks like a hammer with legs and is immediately to the left of the hand clap. Because we want a beat that's not too fast or too slow, let's add our snare to the middle circle, the one with 8 dots. Drag a snare icon to each of the 8 dots.

Now we have our basic beat. *Dum, dum, dum, dum, dum, dum, dum, dum.* It provides a simple rhythm for us to build on. But this beat alone is pretty boring. Let's add a little swing to make it more cheerful. We don't have to put sounds on the dots. Try adding a snare right before one of the snares we already have.

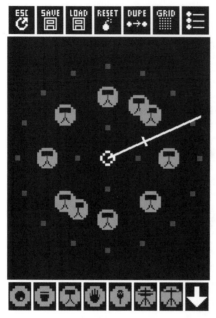

Adding more snare drums

That gives the piece a cool little kick. You can see in the figure that I added two of the snare drums at opposite sides of the circle. Now they'll come in twice per loop, every 8 steps (or every 4 drum beats). *Dum, dum, dum, dah-dum, dum, dum, dum, dah-dum.* That divides our loop into two halves, which gives us a good starting place to add more sounds.

Adding More Sounds

Our loop has two parts, each with its own *dah-dum*. Now we can start to set the two halves apart from each other. Let's add a couple more sounds.

You can play multiple sounds at the same time. We still haven't put anything in the outer ring. If we put two notes next to each other in the outer ring, they'll play faster than the drumbeat in the inner ring. Pick two different sounds and add them to the loop. After the *dah-dum* is a good place. We use the hand clap and the cymbals here.

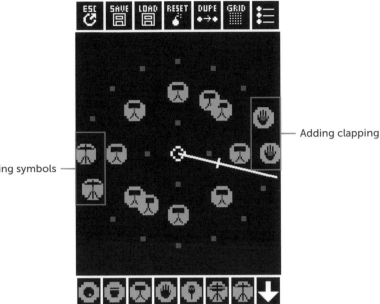

Adding symbols

Adding clapping

Adding even more sounds

These help to build up the percussive sound of our loop. *Percussion* refers to instruments like drums, cymbals, and cowbells, or things you play by hitting them to create rhythm. Now let's add some other instruments on top of them.

Click the arrow to see more of Drumcircle's banks of sounds. You'll find piano notes (in a rainbow of colors representing different scales), guitar notes, and other sounds effects. Some of my favorites include the trash can, computer, and electric guitar.

Each instrument has a different characteristic. Click the acoustic guitar, rock guitar, and metal guitar (they're on the fifth page after the rainbow circles, the one with the dog) and listen to how they sound. The acoustic guitar sounds warm and open, the rock guitar sounds harsh and fast, and the metal guitar (the one with the little skull) sounds low and nasty, almost like a wolf snarling.

Let's add some warmer instruments to our loop.

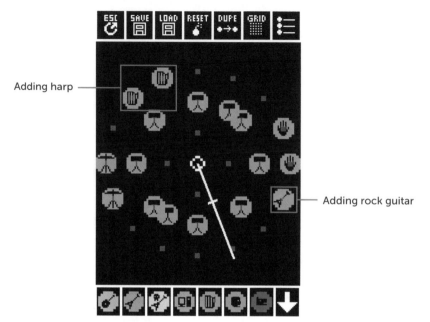

Adding harp

Adding rock guitar

Adding harps and a guitar

Here, we added two harp sounds leading into one of the *dah-dums*, and then a rock guitar sound following the hand claps. Always think about how your sounds will relate to other sounds around it.

Adding a Melody

Now, let's add a melody! We have three different instruments that can be played at multiple scales: the empty rainbow circles sound chippy and bright, the piano keys sound warm and light, and the guitar strums sound bouncy and fun.

We'll use the piano keys because the lower keys are warm and lingering. You can hear the sounds trail off slowly and blend into each other well. We'll also add three notes in a row, rising in scale, which is called a *progression* in music.

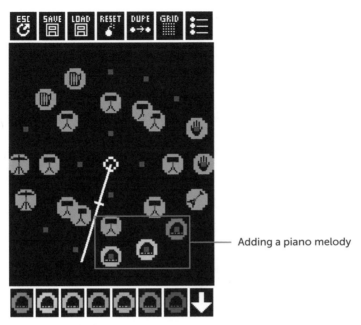

Adding a piano melody

Adding a melody

Because each note is higher than the last, it sounds like the melody is rising. If you're not sure what kind of melody to write, progressions are always a good place to start because they usually sound nice. But you can experiment with playing notes in different sequences. Can you make a loop that sounds sad? Or tense? Or silly?

Saving and Exporting Loops

Click the **Save** button at the top of the window, and you'll see eight different slots to save loops to. As in Audacity and sfxr, saving your work and exporting your work are different processes. By saving a loop, you can load it and edit it more later. The Export Wav button is also in the Save menu. As mentioned earlier, Export Wav creates a file that you can use in your games. (The file be named *output1.wav* or *output2.wav*, and so on.) When you're exporting a *WAV* file, keep in mind that the first note is always the one at the top (where 12 would be on a clock).

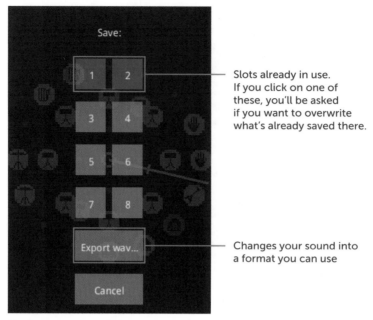

Slots already in use. If you click on one of these, you'll be asked if you want to overwrite what's already saved there.

Changes your sound into a format you can use

Saving your drum loop

Now open your loop's *WAV* file in Audacity. What does the waveform look like? (Hold down SHIFT before you click Play to make your sound loop.)

What your drum loop looks like in waveform

You could create a song just by stringing together a bunch of different Drumcircle *WAV* files in Audacity.

Bosca Ceoil

If you really like and feel comfortable with music sequencing, you might want to try Bosca Ceoil. Named after an Irish word for "music box," Bosca Ceoil is a simple, free, music-making tool created by Terry Cavanagh.

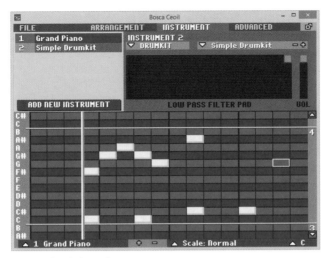

Bosca Ceoil interface

Bosca Ceoil is a bit more complicated than Drumcircle, but it has many more features if you really want to make songs. There are lots of different instruments to work with, and you can make multiple 16-step patterns and chain them together to create a longer song. Bosca Ceoil has an excellent built-in tutorial that will teach you the basics. You can download Bosca Ceoil at *https://boscaceoil.net/*.

Adding a Music Loop to a Scratch Game

A basic music loop in Scratch looks like this.

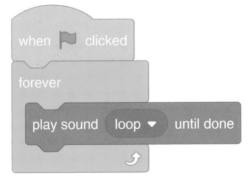

Programming a music loop in Scratch

If you use a plain old play sound block inside a forever loop, it would just keep starting the sound over again. It would be just like the bug's leaf-munching sound that didn't wait to play the entire sound before looping. Terrible!

If you don't want the same song to loop endlessly during your *entire* game, use a repeat until loop instead.

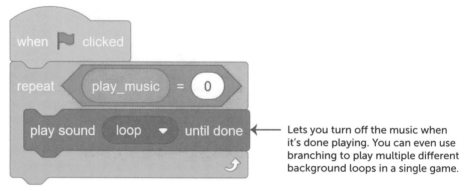

Lets you turn off the music when it's done playing. You can even use branching to play multiple different background loops in a single game.

Turning off the music after the song ends

It's also handy to know that Scratch's Sound Library comes with a whole bunch of premade loops that you can use. Check out these loops in the Music Loops category!

![Premade music loops in Scratch showing a Choose a Sound library with rows of speaker icons labeled: Bossa Nova, Cave, Chill, Classical Pi..., Cymbal Echo, Dance Aro..., Dance Cel..., Dance Chill..., Dance Ene..., Dance Funky, Dance Hea..., Dance Magic, Dance Sitar, Dance Slo..., Dance Snar..., Dance Space, Drip Drop, Drive Around, Drum, Drum Funky, Drum Jam, Drum Mach..., Drum Satel..., Drum Set1, Drum Set2, Dubstep, Eggs, Elec Piano..., Emotional..., Garden, Guitar Chor..., Guitar Chor..., Hip Hop, Human Be..., Human Be..., Jungle]

Premade music loops in Scratch

NOTE: The loops used in the beginning and ending of *Hatlight* are "Dance Slow Mo" and "Dance Chill Out," respectively.

Keep in mind that you can also edit a sound directly in Scratch. You can't make as many changes as you can in Audacity, but you can adjust the volume and make a sound fade in or out. Fade in and fade out work the same in Scratch as they do in Audacity.

Extra Challenges

If you're ready to take on some challenges, the following sections provide some extra ideas for you to try.

Compose a Score for a Game Using Only Mouth Sounds

There is a huge range of sounds you can make if you experiment: humming noises, farting noises, explosion noises, tongue-clicking noises, or just saying made-up words. Recall that the sound effect for jumping in *Hatlight* was me saying "Hup!" into a mic. If you're feeling ambitious, try to make music for your game entirely with your mouth.

Use Music to Create a Contrasting Mood

Dissonance is a word for the unsettling feeling you get when what you're seeing tells you one thing but what you're hearing tells you another. How would you feel while playing a game in which you run and jump through a bright, happy forest while sinister, scary music plays? How would you feel during a game where your character moves slowly and sadly while happy, poppy music plays? What kinds of weird feelings can you create in your game?

Create a Procedural Music Game

Go to *https://freesound.org/* and find a recording of someone playing lots of notes on an instrument. Use Audacity to cut out four different notes. Play one of those notes when the player moves up, another when they move right, another when they move left, and another when they move down. When the player moves around your game, they will be involuntarily creating music!

What other ways can you come up with to use sound and music in your games?

What You Learned

In this chapter, you learned how to add cool sound effects to convey information to your players and set the right tone for your games. You used Audacity to record and edit your own sound effects, generated sounds using sfxr, and created drum loops using Drumcircle.

In the next and last chapter, I'll share some advice on how to use what you learned in this book to bring your ideas to life.

6

Where to Go from Here

You made it to the last chapter! How does it feel to be a game designer? a little weird? Don't worry—that's normal. Maybe you're saying, "I don't *feel* like a game designer yet," but this book can't hear you. It doesn't have ears.

It's easy to feel like you're not qualified to call yourself something, because labels are tricky. Some game designers work in big teams, and everyone contributes a small part of the finished game. Other game designers sit in their bedrooms making fun things on their computer. Still other game designers go to the park to play catch with friends and come up with different ways of playing, such as saying "What if we have to toss the ball under our leg?" or "What if we're not allowed to touch the ball with our hands?" There are loads of different ways to be a game designer.

Asking Questions

You might not have a ton of game design experience yet, but I'll let you in on a cool fact about game design: if you're doing it right, it should always be a bit of a challenge. Even people who've designed games for years still ask questions: "What if you can only move one space every day?" "What kind of game can you play at a protest?" "Why don't games let you make friends with the monsters instead of fighting them?"

Game design is less about finding answers than it is about asking questions. Everyone, regardless of their skill level and experience, can ask questions.

In this chapter, I provide you with a collection of exercise challenges to make a game in a new way. Some of them will help promote your games and work with others. Each of them is a question that, hopefully, leads you to ask your own questions.

You don't have to do all of the exercises or do them in order. Just do the ones that inspire you the most.

Record Your Game

You also record a video of your game, so you can show off what your game sounds and looks like.

You can use OBS (Open Broadcaster Software) Studio at *https://obsproject.com/* to capture, edit, and upload a record video of your game. It's a free program for streaming game video live, but you can also use it to record video. Then you can post your video on YouTube or social media. The OBS Studio website contains information on how to get started.

Dealing with Online Feedback

When you post things online, you might receive comments and feedback that can be mean-spirited and hurtful. At the same time, you want to be open to feedback that helps you improve your game and your skills. It's important to know the difference between constructive criticism and just plain hating.

Constructive feedback comes from a person who genuinely wants to help you improve. It might be something like, "I really liked *this part*, but *that part* didn't really work for me," or "I found a bug when I tried to do *this*." You can usually identify constructive feedback because it mentions a specific thing that you could fix or improve. It gives you something concrete to work on.

Being online can make you want to develop a thick skin to protect yourself from hurtful people, but try to keep an open mind to those who sincerely want to help you. Also, make sure that when you're commenting on other people's work, you're being helpful and positive too.

Share Your Game on itch.io

The website *https://itch.io/* is full of hundreds of games. Some people use *itch.io* to sell their games, and some people give their games away for free. Having your game on *itch.io* means that people will find it more easily. Now that you know how to make a *gif* file or video of your game, you can use that footage to show people browsing *itch.io* what your game looks like.

On *itch.io*, players can either download your game to their computer or play it on the site. To let players play your game on *itch.io*, you'll need to embed it on *itch.io*. You can find an explanation of how to embed a Scratch game on the Scratch wiki at *http://tinyurl.com/scratchio/*.

Posting a game on *itch.io* makes you part of a larger community of game creators and can help your game find a larger audience. Becoming brave enough to put your work out into the larger world is an important part of becoming a powerful artist.

Collaborate with Someone Else

Try making a game with a friend. It can be very exciting to bounce ideas back and forth with someone else, each of you building on what the other comes up with. Some of the most powerful ideas happen that way, and the energy of collaboration can be lots of fun.

You can work together on a project in many different ways. Maybe the other person draws all the pictures and you do the programming. Or maybe you both come up with as many ideas as possible and include all of them. Maybe the other person just hangs with you while you work and tries to give you cool ideas.

Working with other people on creative projects can be tricky, especially when they're friends. If you get into an argument about the project, it could affect your friendship. Collaborating feels great when you both have the same level of energy and excitement, but tensions can build when you both have different amounts of energy or availability. Sometimes it might feel like one person takes charge of the whole project and makes all the decisions.

Collaboration is all about communication! If someone doesn't feel like they're involved enough in decision-making or feels frustrated because they think they're spending more time on the project than the other person, have a conversation about it! Try not to get defensive. Think about constructive criticism: try to be specific about what the problem is, how it makes you feel, and what could make the situation better.

Collaboration is a lot of work, but it will lead to amazing things you couldn't make on your own.

Make a Game for Multiple Players

Playing a game by yourself with a computer can be surprising and fun, but playing a game with another person can be even more enjoyable. When you play a game with someone else, you're not just playing according to the rules of the game. You're also trying to anticipate, respond to, or make sense of what the other player is doing. Try making a game for two (or more!) players.

Players interact in many different ways. They can each be *competing* to get the high score, to get to the flag first, or to knock the other player off the giant marshmallow. Or they could be *cooperating* to try to accomplish the same thing. Maybe they need to work together to steer a giant robot (one player controls the legs while the other player controls the arms). Or maybe your game could be a mix of competition and cooperation.

How do you add a second player? So far, we've had the player use the arrow keys to move their character. But Scratch lets us write code for any keyboard key. You can add a second (or third or fourth) player by giving them other keys to play the game with!

Traditionally, game developers use the WASD keys. They're arranged in the same way as the arrow keys if you think of W as up, A as left, S as down, and D as right. They're also on the opposite side of the keyboard from the arrow keys, giving both players some room.

What if you put both players' buttons really close to each other? How would that change how the players interact?

Make a Weird Controller

There are a lot of ideas we've seen so many times that we take them for granted. In Scratch's keyboard **Sensing** block, the arrow keys are at the very top of the list. But if you have access to video game consoles, how could you move a character using the controller? There's probably either a d-pad with arrows or a stick that can point in different directions.

Just because people usually do things one way doesn't mean it's the only way to do it (or even the best way!). A controller can look like anything. If you made a game about learning to walk in a strange, new robot body, would it make sense for the controls to be familiar? The way we control a game is part of the game's experience. Try to imagine controls that match what the game's experience is supposed to be.

Here are a couple ideas for reimagining game controls:

Mod an existing controller. You can use lots of simple objects to change the experience of using a keyboard or mouse. What about a game where the player's been shrunk? Instead of being next to each other, the keys for moving around can be far across the keyboard from each other. You can make an overlay for the keyboard that has holes for just those keys.

Or how about a game where the player tries to get around a space station in zero gravity by pushing off the walls and ceiling? You could hang the mouse in the center of a cardboard box (its cord dangling through a hole in the top) so the player needs to find somewhere on the side or top of the box to move the mouse against. It would be a game about a mouse, controlled using the mouse, and you could put little ears on the computer mouse so it looks like a real mouse. The possibilities are limited only by your arts and crafts supplies!

Make an object into a controller. An invention called the Makey Makey lets you press keys on your keyboard by touching objects in your house. You can check it out (and buy one) at *https://makeymakey.com/*.

The Makey Makey Go is cheap and fits in a pocket. Plug it into your computer, and then run a wire from it to any object that's *conductive,* which means something that conducts electricity. Most objects in your house that are either metal or contain water (like fruits, plants, or food) are conductive.

You can turn the following conductive objects into a game controller:

- A banana or other fruit
- A leaf or plant
- Aluminum foil
- Coins, paper clips, or metal washers
- A slice of bread
- Modeling clay

When you touch the object plugged into the Makey Makey, it registers a mouse click or spacebar press on your computer. What kind of game would you play on a piece of bread or a ball of aluminum foil?

If you want to use a bunch of different objects to control your game, you might get a Makey Makey Classic. It costs a bit more, but it comes with enough wires to connect six different objects. Try making a new controller for one of your favorite games.

Keep Exploring and Creating!

Most important is to explore and be creative. Making art—whether that's games, comics, zines, music, writing, or just a little garden in your window—helps you realize what you're capable of. It leads you to feel wonder for yourself and your surroundings.

The older you get, the less time you have for play and creating things that don't make money. Get in the habit of making and doing, and hold onto it as you grow older! It's never too late to start. Making art will increase your enjoyment for life. *For real.*

Congratulations on finishing the book! But this book is just a starting point. Now that you know how to make games using Scratch, it's up to you to figure out what to do with that knowledge. Follow your ideas wherever they lead, even if they seem silly, weird, or unoriginal. Keep exploring. I can't wait to see what you come up with.

Index